Seven Roads to Glory

Published by Empower Productions, Inc.
Woodstock, Georgia 30188
www.drcarolynporter.com

© 2007 by Carolyn Porter

All rights reserved. No part of this book may be reproduced in any form or by any means without permission in writing from the author.

First printing: November 2007

Library of Congress Control Number: 2007907232

ISBN-13: 978-0-9711150-8-8
ISBN-10: 0-9711150-8-7

Printed at Walsworth Printing Company through
Four Colour Imports, Ltd.

Book design by Jill Anderson, www.JillLynnDesign.com
Edited by Susan Grimm

Seven Roads to Glory

POWERFUL STORIES OF INCREDIBLE CHALLENGES AND HOW TO BECOME THE VICTOR!

Carolyn Porter, D. Div.

ALSO BY CAROLYN PORTER, D. DIV.

BOOKS

A Woman's Path to Wholeness
The Realness of a Woman
What Are You Saying?
Healing with Color
Angel Love
101 Great Ways to Improve Your Life (co-author)

AUDIO BOOKS

Grab Your Authentic Power
Healthier & Younger: Turn Back the Clock
Healing with Color Meditation Audio

All of the above are available at your local bookstore, or can be ordered by visiting www.drcarolynporter.com.

*To the many hurting hearts
who long to know there is hope.*

With Deepest Gratitude

To God and the Angels for placing the desire to put this book together so that many can find the hope to move through their challenge to glory.

To the seven people who are willing to share their story with the world so that hearts can be touched and lives healed.

To the families and friends who have been there for these seven people, supporting and loving them through their challenging journey.

To Jill, who listened to my ideas and with passion created the wonderful designs for this book.

To Susan, for sharing her editing abilities.

Contents

Preface
11

ONE | Let Me Introduce You to Harry,
a Human Being Extraordinaire
21

TWO | About Anita, written by Anita
43

THREE | Rick's Collection of Stories,
written by Rick Beneteau
89

FOUR | Carolyn's Life Reflection
135

FIVE | This is Danielle
161

SIX | From Beverly's Heart
203

SEVEN | And Now Kate's Story
235

Afterword
261

About the Author
270

Preface

Every human being living on this planet has a story. Most are living in their story right now, creating their life according to their thoughts and beliefs. Many do not like the story they are creating yet have no idea that all they need do is step out of their story and begin living life as they desire it to be.

My old story presented aspects I certainly didn't like. I experienced a rigid, controlled childhood, a long unhappy marriage although it produced five wonderful children (they are my greatest gifts!), a continual struggle with low self-worth, illness that took five years to heal, near financial ruin from an unethical business partner, and so on. Life to me was hard, and a struggle to come up for air at times.

Each of you reading this book has your own story. Perhaps your story includes hardships, challenges, problems, struggle, or the various road blocks that come to everyone at some point in their life. What I have come to understand is that we have the power of choice, that we don't have to remain in the old story, and that we actually have the power to remove ourselves from the story and begin living our dreams. In addition, I have learned that every challenge that comes our way is a gift from God, and that the entire scenario could be changed if we realized this one important fact of life: We all have problems, but it's in how we see them and grow through them that makes the difference between becoming a victim or a victor. Our greatest power in this world is the power of choice! Instead of being the effect of life's circumstances—the old story of pain, hurt, struggle, lack—you actually have the power to step out of it and become a creator of something exciting and glorious.

Oprah Winfrey, who most assuredly is an example of receiving the desires of her heart and then some, was once fired as a reporter and given a shot of projected doom, a very unhealthy set-up for failure from her employer. Instead of accepting that as a truth, she stepped away from that negative perception and created what she envisioned as her truth—that she could be more. She said, "I live in the space of thankfulness—and I have been rewarded a million times over for it. I started out giving thanks for the small things, and the more thankful I became, the more my bounty increased. That's because what you focus on expands, and when you focus on the goodness in your life, you create more of it. Opportunities, relationships, even money flowed my way when I learned to be grateful no matter what happened in my life."

As you read the stories of these ordinary people and how they stepped right through what seemed to be insurmountable difficulties, understand that you can overcome any challenges you are presently facing as well. You can choose whether you will participate in a continual "pity party" or squeeze those perceived sour lemons into wonderful, sweet lemonade! There is always a bigger picture then what you can see or understand at first, for the gift may not be visible at first glance. However, if you have faith and make the choice to step out of your story—the pain, hurt, anger, guilt, shame, lack, or whatever negative feelings you are experiencing—focus on the good in your life and be continually grateful for it, your life can become a glorious, exciting adventure, even as you are walking through the challenge. It's simple: Make lemonade from your lemons!

SYNCHRONICITY—
THE EVOLUTION OF THIS BOOK

Before this book was even a thought, I met a man named *Harry*. He is a recording engineer and I was in need of just such a person. He frequented the church I attend which was where we were introduced. During our initial conversation, I discovered his vocation and, since I needed to record and create an audio, knew I had been led in his direction for this meeting.

As we worked together on that first audio I was so impressed with his heart, and even more so after hearing his story of how he turned tragedy to triumph. I commented that he should share his story to show others they can overcome the struggles and difficulties of their life, you know, the old cliché of "If he can do it, then maybe I can." He replied that he knew this but had no idea where to begin. That was the *aha* moment when I realized that he and I had connected to support each other since I am an author and knew the ropes of self-publishing a book. He agreed to begin recording his information so I could transcribe it into his story.

In the meantime, I created a short version of part of his story and placed it on my website. Apparently, it showed up when someone did a search on Google for his name, and thus began the procession of people wanting to hear his complete story. Time lapsed, and a busy schedule (resistance) prevented him from finishing the recording. More time went by and still resistance continued. Then one day, during my meditation time, I was guided in a different direction. I was guided to put the book together myself and include several stories of people who stepped through their horrific challenges and triumphed. This would be much easier for each person since no one would have to go through the process of writing an entire book alone. My mind was whirling as I internalized this idea and I excitedly called Harry. The idea clicked with him so I placed an intention out to the universe for the other stories to show up. Here's what happened.

The first three people I approached about this were initially interested but changed their mind shortly thereafter. Bummer! Now what was I to do? I surrendered the search, realizing that I needed to get out of the way so that the right and perfect people could show up. After all, this was a God project! A few months later, while participating in a mini national marketing campaign, I was interviewed by a radio host located in Florida. A few days after the interview she connected me with a high school student who had questions about publishing a book. The student emailed me with her questions and we connected. She asked if I would read her first chapter, and when I did, chills showed up (a signal to pay attention to this). I had the feeling this was another story. I introduced this idea to *Anita,* the student, and she loved the idea. Wow! Now there are two stories. The synchronicity of everything in life is so awesome when your spirit is aligned with purpose; everything simply flows to you with ease!

Just before my connection with Anita, I received an email introducing me to an interesting campaign called The Happiness Campaign. It intrigued me and, after speaking with the founder, I joined.

Little did I know the connection with this man would put me in touch with another person with a story to tell. When the email came it simply said this: Carolyn, meet Rick. Rick, meet Carolyn. The rest is history. *Rick* and I talked and he resonated with the book idea, so willingly agreed to participate. Story number three! See how it all works? It simply flows to you effortlessly when you are in alignment with spirit!

Three great stories yet there were more to come. So I waited. Two more people agreed to participate but then withdrew, so I waited some more. No one appeared with a story to share. (I believe in the Law of Attraction—Place an intention to the universe and you will attract that desire, without doing anything to make it happen.) I began to question my guidance, thinking three stories were fine. It was then that the message came through loud and clear that I was to share my story as well; I was to be story number four. This had not been in my plan, yet I realized that the plan for this book was much greater than I could grasp in the beginning. Although my original guidance seemed to indicate there would be three stories, I was being guided that seven would be best. That meant I still needed three more stories. So I waited.

Where Miracles Happen, my healing center, had opened and was attracting those who needed help on life's journey. One day *Danielle* walked in distraught and obviously in pain, and asking for help. As she shared some of her story with me a rush of chills went through me. I felt strongly this could very well be another story. And it is!

Two more stories were still to come. Patience I was told—just wait quietly. One day, out of the blue, one of the original people I had asked to share her story called. Some obstacles that had appeared months before were no longer in the way. She thought the book was already completed, but I informed her that two more stories were coming. Without any hesitation *Beverly* said, "I'm ready now. The timing is right. I'd like to be part of the book." Okay, that made six—only one more to go.

A woman had shared her story, story number seven, and the book was completely finished. But wait! Without notice this woman decided it wasn't the right time for her to be part of our book. Now what? It felt like a major dilemma with the time crunch of final preparations. Then I remembered, and put into practice the principles represented in this book. I surrendered the situation and knew there would be a perfect outcome. I mentioned what had happened to a friend who then mentioned *Kate*, saying she had a story to share. Kate felt honored to share it and within hours she became story number seven!

So there you have it—the complete orchestration of how the universe works to bring together the right and perfect outcome for any possibility, without any effort on our part if we simply get out of the way and allow it to flow to us!

As for the title—Each of the seven people included in this book are journeying on their own path. Each story is unique, yet each one exemplifies similar characteristics and principles that enabled triumph over their challenge. Each story is their truth shared simply to offer hope and encouragement for you, so you know you can conquer anything. Glory is simply a condition of highest achievement, something of which each individual can be very proud. In my comprehension, there is no achievement greater than overcoming what has been deemed impossible and moving forward and upward through it!

Open you heart and mind and join us on the Road to Glory. And so it is . . .

1

LET ME INTRODUCE YOU TO HARRY

Let Me Introduce You to Harry, a Human Being Extraordinaire

Dedicated to God, my family, my friends,
and the awesome power of true love.

It was a beautiful fall day in early October, October 3, 1983 to be exact. The sun was high in the sky, brilliantly shining as the crisp coolness of autumn filled the air. The day had presented only wonderful visions of fantastic possibilities.

Life was good; that's what Harry thought. He was quite content. He and his wife were happy together and he was doing the things he loved to do: rebuilding older cars, playing bass guitar in a traveling band, and technical assistant in a recording company. He loved playing music and loved to dance, and he was good at both. As Harry drove away from his morning meeting, he was smiling as he sang along with the music that floated to his ears from his car radio. He was en route to see about purchasing another "over the hill" car, a Trans Am to be exact, so he could fix her up. He loved cars!

Happily cruising as he hummed the radio tunes, he noticed a car sitting by the roadside with a man looking under the hood. As the man heard Harry's car approaching he began waving his arms to attract attention to his dilemma. Harry immediately signaled to pull off the road to see if he could help this man in distress, especially since fixing ailing cars was one of his specialties. The man was obviously overjoyed to see help arrive and asked Harry if he would jumpstart the car. Harry hooked up the cables between both cars and was in the process of priming the man's carburetor. He tried three times with no success, but suggested they try one more time. He was standing in front of the man's car, priming the carburetor, hoping he'd have this guy on his way in short order, when suddenly, in a split second, his life abruptly ended as it had been.

Harry was born in a Valdosta, Georgia on January 10, 1956. His dad was in the Air Force where he met Harry's mother, who happened to be visiting her sister. The attraction was strong and they soon married. A year later Harry was born. Soon after they moved to New York, Harry was joined by two brothers. The three brothers, each a year apart, fought like cats and dogs as siblings often do, but later became quite close.

When he was in fourth grade, Harry's family moved to a small town in upstate New York. Sports were big for Harry and became a major focus through many school years. Baseball was a main love until his interest shifted to music. During high school he joined the school band, playing the trumpet, but eventually gravitated toward the bass guitar, which led him to join a band. It was about that time the Beatles hit the limelight and Harry loved their music. When he was thirteen he took part in the Woodstock Festival in New York and was amazed at the throngs of people that were present; he had

Let Me Introduce You to Harry

never seen so many in one place before. He was especially amazed at so many longhaired individuals!

Harry's dad was an entertainer and often drank with his buddies. Over time, this habit developed into a heavy drinking problem and eventually led to the breakup of their family. His mom moved to Georgia to be near her family. When she left it tore Harry and his brothers up and everything changed dramatically after that.

At 16, a junior in high school, Harry moved out on his own and stayed with a guitar player and his wife for two years. His dad had moved out of the school district where he had been going to school, but Harry wanted to graduate with his friends. The couple was kind enough to provide a place for Harry so he could remain with his friends. It also was a way for him to remain close to his high school sweetheart, Cindy.

God was not in the picture for Harry; he had turned his back on God. He figured that if God would cause his family to break up he didn't want anything to do with God. Lots of partying, lots of drinking, lots of fun became Harry's lifestyle during the years from fourteen through nineteen. It seemed to be acceptable to drink; many parents allowed their kids to drink thinking they were at least at home and not out on the streets. Small town, lots of woods, and parents said "If you're going to drink then do it here where we know where you are." Harry simply followed in his father's footsteps.

After graduation Harry moved down to Georgia with his mom. He met a singer named Alicia Bridges who hired him to rehearse with her. They'd practice songs and then record them. Limos picked them up and they were groomed—clothing, hair, movements—according to certain requirements. Harry loved it! Alicia released a single hit song called "I Love the Night Life" during this time. Harry continued to work with her for the summer but he was homesick. He missed his friends and his old band wanted him to come back to New York. They had played together since he was about fourteen. So Harry headed back north as fall approached.

Harry's drinking continued and so did the party life. It seemed natural for Harry to slide in next to his dad and become part of the entertainment scene. They began playing together, and then there would be parties and drinking after or between the shows. A couple buddies of his came back from the army and they all went on a three-day binge during which Harry found himself blacked out in New York City. Blackouts continued and this scared him enough that he wanted to make some changes, for he knew that blackouts were a symptom of alcoholism.

Shortly before this his dad had decided that after all these years it was time for him to sober up. He had joined a self-help group and became sober. Once again, Harry decided to follow in his dad's footsteps. This time it was a better choice.

Harry told me "I'll never forget that day—September 8, 1975. It was total surrender. I knew what I was doing just wasn't working. I had a tremendous peace come over me that day. It was a turning point for me, a day I will always remember." He joined the self-help group as his dad had done, letting go of the years of self-destruction.

Remaining in New York for another year, H̶ unthinkable—he became a bartender! Sobriety and baring are like trying to mix oil and water; watching everyone getting drunk just didn't help his resolve to remain sober. So he soon quit that job and began to chauffeur a gangster around for a while, one who loved to drink—still playing with fire wasn't he? Finally, it was time—time for change and a different life. Again, he moved back to Georgia to be near his mom, and shortly thereafter brought his girlfriend, Debbie Perry, to join him. She was important in his life for the next five years.

Moving on to a new phase of life, Harry worked at Big Star Foods for a couple years, bought a condo for he and Debbie, and felt things were going along pretty well. Then he met a man named Bob Burns who had played with the Lynyrd Skynyrd Band. Bob asked, "Why don't we put a band together?" That's exactly what they did. Harry quit working at Big Star and began traveling, touring the southeast, including Florida. Harry traveled with the band for three years and it was a time of growing up for Harry. He realized for the first time that it didn't matter where he was, home was in the heart. Bob was good for him because he'd been all around the world by the time Harry came on the scene so he taught Harry a lot about life, especially how to lighten up and enjoy life. Bob wanted everyone to smile and be happy which is exactly what Harry needed to learn. However, the traveling was taking its toll on his relationship with Debbie and he began to experience burn-out, so he decided to get off the road. In the end, Debbie left and went back to New York.

Bob found a local gig in Atlanta, and the plan was to remain local, no more traveling. It was a club called Ease On In, and they soon discovered it was a rough, gun-slinging club. One night two women began fighting over a pistol and who was going to shoot whom. The club cleared fast leaving the band on stage playing as these women scuffled with the gun. It wasn't unusual for the band to be left on stage playing when a few people began waving guns after everyone cleared out in a flash. It was time for them to move on to something better and back on the road it was.

As Harry and the band traveled through various cities, one city became important to Harry. In Johnson City, Tennessee, lived one particular female named Karen. In 1980 she became his wife and Harry got off the road again. He and Bob started a Contemporary Christian band since Bob was religious, and they performed together for about a year. Harry was confused about God, not knowing what he really believed, but somehow he ended up at Mt. Paran Church in Atlanta where he really connected with the minister named Dr. Walker, also a musician. What appealed to Harry was that this man spoke from the heart, having been through struggles of his own, he could relate to those who had been hurt. Harry found God again.

On to another job—construction—with long hours and long hair. Here he met a couple great guys, Tom Deel and Roger Gossett. Now Tom was one of those guys who would get in your face and push your buttons, but he was extremely intelligent and would blow you away with what he could figure in his head. So Harry began praying for a shield of protection around himself and mercy for Tom. One day, as Tom was screaming in Harry's face, Harry kept praying and blessing Tom, asking for a shield of protection again. Tom suddenly stopped and got quiet. This freaked Harry out as he realized his prayers were actually working. From that moment on their relationship shifted into one of mutual understanding with a friendly atmosphere in the workplace. Respect for Harry emerged from Tom, and Harry was now a believer in the Power of Prayer! Later Tom was instrumental in providing a job that brought Harry back into music, his real love.

Back to music and soon on the road again, even though the promise had been to Karen and himself to remain in local areas. A year of traveling was putting a strain on his marriage and after reading a book on how to have a good marriage, Harry knew he had to put his wife first. That meant getting off the road. And he stayed off the road.

A recording studio owner named Jerry Gibson hired Harry to be a manager of the studio. He continued playing bass in a band with Bob Burns. Writing songs, practicing all day, recording at night, and producing recordings became his way of life. And then anniversary time—8 years of sobriety on September 8, 1983!

Move forward now to October 3, 1983; Harry's life would never be the same again. As he was priming the man's carburetor for the fourth time, the man decided to crank the engine before Harry got his head out from under the hood, even though he'd told him to wait until he gave the signal. An explosion ripped through the air and flames shot out from under the hood, engulfing Harry's shoulders, face and head in flames, also exploding the gas can he held in his hands. He tried to put out the flames with his hands but when it didn't work, he remembered the creek he'd seen as he approached the stricken car. With his flesh searing under the intense heat of the soaring flames, he ran for the creek. He felt the edge with his hands and bent over to put his head in thinking the water was shallow. Instead, as he dropped his body into the water, he discovered there was an eight foot drop. Coming down on a rock he heard his neck crack, and the flames that were burning his shoulders, head, hands and face extinguished themselves.

Harry's legs came over his head; he had no control over them. As he felt his body begin moving downstream with the current he tried to stop his movement with his arm. But he was losing control of that as well. He told himself, "No, you can't lose control of your arm" as he planted it into the creek dirt. His stomach muscles were losing control now and his breathing became more difficult as his chest tightened. Over and over he tried to get up, but he couldn't. He thought, "I'm 28 years old, in great shape with my regular running and weight lifting, I can shake this off." But numbness overtook his body and he felt strange, like the feeling if you hammered your finger on accident—that same numbness.

Harry glanced up the hill. The man whom he had been helping stood there absolutely frozen in place, his car behind him all ablaze with flames shooting high into the air. Harry mouthed the words to go get some help, but without his stomach muscles he doubts if any sound came out of his mouth. At that point he wondered if he'd ever get out of the creek. Was he on his way out of life? He noticed how blue the sky was, how beautiful and sunny, and the trees that rustled gently above him. As he was taking this in a tremendous feeling of peace suddenly enveloped him. It was as if heaven itself was embracing him. Then he heard a voice say, "Harry, you're going to learn more about yourself than you could have learned in an entire lifetime." Harry remembers thinking this was the craziest thought given where he was. Here he was, lying in this creek, not knowing if he was ever going to get out of it alive, when an exhilarating feeling of excitement overtook him. It was like the feeling a kid has on Christmas morning. He thought, "Geez, this is absolutely nuts!" Then he thought about his wife and his family and prayed they'd be okay. He knew it would hurt them all if he left this life.

Harry's thoughts were suddenly interrupted when a man jumped down in the hole with him, a passer-by who assessed the situation and saw help was needed. He began asking Harry his name, social security number and ways of identification, shouting to the people standing on the hill to call an ambulance immediately. This man stayed with Harry until the ambulance came, with Harry fully conscious the entire time.

As Harry was experiencing his body on fire, he said he felt as if he was watching a movie about someone else, that although he was in motion, it didn't feel it was him. It didn't make sense to him but that's what it felt like. He felt like the Observer even though he had no idea what that was then. His body was out of control but there was something watching this in action, something watching this machine (his body) react.

Excruciating pain enveloped Harry—burns to his face and head, bloody, bruised, burned, soaked to the skin and his head in agonizing pain. Rushed to the Smyrna Hospital for emergency treatment, he was then immediately taken by ambulance to Northside Hospital and placed in the Intensive Care Unit. His wife was in shock upon seeing him in the emergency room. How fast life can change in one split second of time.

Not expected to live, but Harry beat the odds. Two weeks in intensive care to stabilize his neck, traction with screws into his head that kept him completely immobile, and agonizing pain that wouldn't ever stop. But there were blessings. Although his face, ear and hair were burned, the healing was fast since he had extinguished the flames so quickly. His neurosurgeon, one of the best in the country, was on hand to do the surgery and told Harry another minute and he'd have lost his eyes from the flames. Staff began letting family and friends in to see him—not the usual for intensive care—but later Harry learned the doctors didn't believe he'd make it so allowed his family and friends to be around him. The people visiting made him feel better, surrounding him with concern and love.

A young boy who had been riding a four-wheeler without a helmet was in intensive care with him. The boy cried out repeatedly, apparently in agony and probably very afraid. Later Harry learned from his dad that the boy didn't make it, which upset Harry, but also made him more determined to make it himself. Harry's dad had flown in from New York to be with him and his mom was nearby as were his brothers. His dad was a changed man now, kind and loving, after years of sobriety.

With his neck finally stabilized, surgery was performed, and he was moved from ICU to a regular room for another week. Then he was transferred to Shepherd Spinal Center where he was again placed into intensive care for an additional two weeks. Physical therapy began and sitting up in a wheel chair was initiated.

Harry was in denial. There is no way this could really be happening to him. He would fight and beat this, whatever it was that had gotten hold of him. Even though the prognosis was paralyzed from the chest down, he would not accept this. But he was so weak and could do nothing for himself. Many thoughts ran through his mind and he found himself in a great emotional upheaval that ran the gamut of anger, depression, why me, and total devastation; this couldn't be for real. He had no energy. Being a man who was in great physical shape before the accident, on the go and an avid musician, this was a tremendous blow. Over the next few months he lost 50 pounds. He couldn't get out of bed or get dressed on his own; he couldn't even turn over or put on his socks without help. He had to be fed because he couldn't feed himself. No way could this be happening to him. No way. He would beat this.

When Harry first glanced in a mirror, he cried out, "Oh my God, I'm a mess!" Face healing from the burns. Hair singed off on one side. Eyebrows gone. Ear burned. But in the midst of all his devastation, he felt great love wrapped around him. So many visitors and friends stopped by, bringing gifts, cards, checks, food, and of course their support and love. One time an elderly couple stopped in for a visit, people he didn't even know. They were teary-eyed and handed him a check, saying they just wanted to visit him and support him during this time. They had heard his story in the media.

One night, he awakened, crying from a powerful dream. Jesus was carrying him. He asked Jesus why this had happened to him. No answer. Jesus just kept walking, carrying him. It was as though Jesus already knew and there was no need for any words. Harry felt a silent strength envelop him. That dream left a profound imprint on him. He knew he was being watched over.

As he was placed in a wheel chair and taken to therapy, Harry would see other people in wheel chairs and immediately think, "I'm not like them." He kept asking for his bass guitar. After all, he'd played that thing every day for the last 10 years. Finally, after repeatedly begging his wife to bring it to him, she did. But he wasn't prepared for what happened and the result knocked him for a loop. He picked up his guitar but couldn't make it work—his fingers simply didn't work the same way any longer. He couldn't even get out one note. He said it blew him out the door and was the second most devastating moment. He remembers crying out to God, "No, not this too. Are you going to take everything away from me? My legs? My independence? And now my music? No God no, not my music!" That anguished moment was a tough one, beyond the expression of human words, and was a crushing blow to his spirit. He wondered if he had what it took to go on anymore.

News media began arriving at Harry's hospital room. Channel 2 and Channel 5 TV crews from Atlanta appeared and interviewed him as well as wrote articles about his tragedy. A trust fund was set up for donations at the First National Bank of Cobb County to help cover the astronomically high medical expenses that were accumulating. Harry had a little insurance but not nearly enough for what he needed to cover his medical expenses. One reporter, Lewis Grizzard, had written his story and the news traveled across the country, alerting people to Harry's situation. One of Grizzard's stories was printed in the Atlanta Journal Constitution on Sunday, October 16, 1983, under the heading of "Good deed turns dream to nightmare," located in the Metro & State section. In this article Grizzard says, "Doctors performed a spinal fusion on Harry O'Brien at Northside Hospital. Now, Harry can raise his arms chest-high, but he's not able to raise his fingers. There is little hope he will ever play his guitar again." A friend is quoted in the same article to say, "Harry wanted to really do something with his music . . . and now those dreams are out there in that ditch. And all he was trying to do was help another person."

Excruciating pain was part of every moment of his life for weeks. Sometimes a nurse would touch him too hard, causing him to scream out with the pain. He was slowly learning to become mobile via the wheel chair. Simple tasks such as lifting a fork to his mouth were impossible, but over time he learned to feed himself again. Once during his healing process a blood clot developed in his leg so Harry was sent back to intensive care for two more weeks. Someone placed a copy of the Prayer of St. Francis on his wall, but the words had no meaning to Harry at that point.

Thanksgiving came and Harry was allowed to go home for a day. This would be a test of how well he could manage out of the hospital on his own. He was home with his wife but it was brutal. She had to care for him and help him with everything. Their apartment had steps so he had to be carried. It was a tough night for both of them because things were so completely different from what either of them had ever imagined. That night, Harry made the decision that it was time to finish up with the Shepherd's Spinal Center and get his life going.

He began wheeling himself up and down the corridors of the clinic, strengthening his arms. He practiced holding his silverware and getting food to his mouth, a tedious and disheartening task at the beginning. It was like learning everything all over again. Harry said, "Imagine putting socks over your hands and tape over your mouth while sitting in a chair. That's what it felt like."

Soon it was Christmas time and that meant a whole week home. Harry's wife had gotten a new apartment that was more accessible by wheelchair. This helped a great deal. Harry was determined to become self-sufficient and independent once again. He continued to build his strength. But there were problems. Eating out was difficult. Often at first he'd drop his fork or even his food. Sometimes he'd actually fall out of the car onto the ground as he was trying to get from the seat to his wheelchair, or the wheelchair would take off with a mind of its own leaving him there in the dust, feeling helpless. It was the little things that seemed to make it so difficult. There was so much fear, yet Harry had an inner knowing that he was being taken care of by a force and power much bigger than he was.

Finally, after four months of hospitals and healing time, Harry went home to stay. He bought a car and had hand controls put on it, allowing him to become more self-reliant. Staring at the fire in his fireplace became a favorite of his and he believes the fire was a big part of his healing of the internal pain from this devastating and life-altering experience. He would stare and think to himself how he was going to do this new life. He often thought of that spiritual experience he had as he was in the creek, knowing God and the angels were watching over him, yet wondering what it meant. As he said, "Fire got me into this place and fire healed me." Pretty powerful, isn't it?

On March 8, 1984, an amazing letter came for Harry. It was written on White House stationary from President Ronald Reagan and Nancy Reagan. They had heard his story and sent him wishes for his recovery and to let him know he was in their prayers. He was cited as a humanitarian who had given so much for his fellowman. Harry has this letter framed and hanging on his wall as one of the most important memories of this time in his life. The letter follows on the next page.

Harry was also nominated in 1984 for the Good Samaritan Reward for Georgia and later that year he met Max Cle-

THE WHITE HOUSE

WASHINGTON

March 8, 1984

Dear Harry:

Word of your unfortunate accident has come to me and I want you to know that Nancy and I are remembering you in our prayers.

Our Nation is greatly blessed to have citizens like you who reach out and help their fellowman. You displayed remarkable concern for another in need last October, and I am proud to commend your fine deed.

I know this is a challenging time for you, but I also understand that you are well-known and admired for your fight and spirit. Our prayer is that those special qualities will help you now and throughout the many years ahead.

May the good Lord always be with you. Please keep up the good fight, and God bless you.

Sincerely,

Ronald Reagan

Mr. Harry O'Brien
Apartment 20E
810 Cherokee Road
Smyrna, Georgia   30080

land, with his own incredible story of survival, who was then the Secretary of State and at this writing is a United States Senator. These were some of the gifts that appeared on Harry's journey that wouldn't have come had he not experienced this horrific trauma.

Now it meant Harry must learn a new trade to support he and his wife. He went to technical school to become an accountant. A man named Jerry Gibson, who owned a recording studio which had hired Harry before to play guitar, suggested Harry learn to be a recording engineer. So he did. After a time someone offered to finance a recording studio for him, and Harry bought Jerry's equipment in 1986, opening his studio in Smyrna, Georgia. Harry was happy to be back in the music arena.

In 1988 Travis Tritt procured Harry's engineering services and the resulting demos got Tritt a record deal with Warner Brothers. In addition, in 1993, Harry recorded a group called Tag Team with a major hit called "Whoomp, There It Is!" It was certified for four million record sales and stayed on the top 40 charts for 43 weeks, the longest running single at that time. It even beat out "The Twist!" Harry has two big plaques on his wall for the amazing status those recordings reached, due, in part, to his recording skills.

Fully independent, Harry decided to move his recording studio to another location in Smyrna. Shortly thereafter, Karen told him she was leaving and wanted a divorce. He knew it was tough for her to care for him, but he didn't see this coming and it was a blow that hit him hard. He was still trying to put his life together. Karen went back to Johnson

City, Tennessee and got a job at an airline reservation desk. It broke his heart because when he married he thought it was for life. However, love was still in their hearts and they continued as friends, visiting back and forth for a year or so. Harry found it tough to travel but did it anyway; he wanted their relationship to work. But Karen wanted him to move back to Johnson City. Harry couldn't see anything for him there and felt deep inside this wasn't a good idea. So, over time, the relationship ended.

Devastated again by another loss, Harry poured himself into his work. On the rebound he discovered another woman whom he met in a restaurant named Kimla. She was a legal secretary and within weeks of their meeting she had moved in with him. Three months later they were married, but the marriage ended a year later.

In 1989 Harry bought his home in Kennesaw, Georgia. He has operated his recording studio from home, but in early 2007 he was able to move it to a new location in Roswell, Georgia. He continues to date some and fill his life with the things he now loves. He still keeps a car he renovated, a 1968 burgundy and black Chevelle Super Sport, and every once in a while you can see him driving it around town.

As I sat across from Harry taping the information you have just read, I couldn't help but marvel at this extraordinary man, so full of love and caring in spite of the horrific challenges he has faced. To many the burden of it all would have beaten them down, perhaps to the point of never surfacing again. But Harry took what he had been given and made something better of it.

He persevered and learned to do the simple things we take for granted—to hold a fork and feed himself, to dress himself, to get his paralyzed body from one place to another, to get out of bed each morning, and even to brush his teeth by himself. He did it all because he determined to do it. He continued to weight train and made his arms strong enough to maneuver his paralyzed body. He manages his home alone and takes care of everything that is possible for him to do. He continues to learn new technology and has become a master recording engineer whose services are sought by many.

As I talked with Harry, I asked him what had impacted his life the most during this process of growing through and overcoming his horrific challenge. He said that what had really touched his heart in a way nothing had ever reached him before, was the power of God that had been unleashed and expressed through the many people who offered him tremendous compassion, love, support and encouragement. He went on to say that never before had he ever experienced the depth of this outpouring from others toward him. They were blessing his life in such a powerful way and he wondered if they had any idea how great their impact had been on his healing process. Moreover, he knew that the power of God through the great magnitude of love of these earth angels is what enabled him to triumph over his situation.

When I asked Harry what finally made him ready to do this taping so I could present his story, this is the story he shared. Since I had asked God and the angels to help Harry see the importance of sharing his story, I am totally convinced they provided this experience to open Harry's eyes and heart!

Harry had gone to Wal-Mart and was nearing his car to go home when he realized another car had parked beside his car so close he couldn't get in with his wheelchair. He was sitting there waiting for someone to help him when he noticed a man approaching him. He called to the man and asked if he could help him a minute. The guy looked at him and said "No." Harry was surprised but continued by saying "Sir, I just need you to move my car back so I can get in." The man said no again. Altogether, Harry called after the man four times asking for his help and the man said no four times while continuing to walk away. As Harry sat there in utter disbelief, he knew he would never be as selfish as that with anyone and was appalled at the heartlessness of this individual. At that moment, he realized his own selfishness in holding back the sharing of his story due to his own busyness. By sharing his story, Harry hopes that others who are hurting, in pain, angry, or challenged by circumstances in their life, will hear his words and invite love in. Thank you angels!

As we closed our time together on the taping day, and were discussing what he wanted people to take away from his story, he said his wish is that someone who is suffering will read his story and simply say, "My God, I can do this too!" And you can!

Epilogue

On December 31, 1998, Harry's mother had a massive heart attack and left this planet. His dad lives near him in Georgia, as do his two brothers. They visit each other often.

Harry told me it is his greatest desire to help others, to be an example of determination and fortitude to get through whatever comes your way and be an inspiration to individuals who need this encouragement. He went on to say that there is tremendous power within us to prevail no matter what is going on around us. There's a bigger picture than what we can physically see. Harry said he's been called to be an example for others to follow.

In support of his sobriety, celebrating 32 years in 2007, Harry supports others as a sponsor while they seek to remove the obstacle of alcohol from their life. Helping others through their healing process has given him great joy. One of Harry's dreams is to attract his soulmate, someone who can open her heart to love, be his friend, companion, supporter, and return the love he gives.

Harry came away from his accident on that day with some amazing realizations. He realized there is something greater out there, something observing his life and yours. He was aware that something is watching; it's silent, and he was able to see birth rather than death. So, his life is about discovering more awareness of that presence that was shown to him on that day. Even now, he often feels as if he's the Observer of his own actions, feeling he isn't real, even though he knows he is. His spirit is soaring higher and higher into greater awareness of who he really is!

You can contact Harry at (770) 591-2221.

2

About Anita

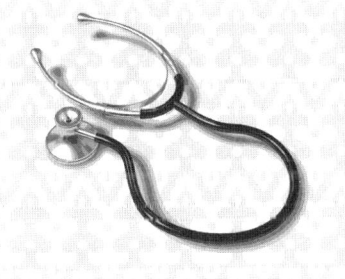

About Anita, written by Anita

Dedicated to God, who has given me the strength to write this, and to my family and friends who have been supportive.

Dear Readers,

When you are a survivor of sexual abuse, you don't scream it from the roof tops or get it tattooed on your forehead. You don't write it down and wear it like a "kick me" sign on your back. As a survivor, I can't shake the hand of someone new that I meet and say, "Hi! My name is Anita and I was molested when I was younger." I can't go on to tell them, "By the way, I have also struggled with depression and anorexia because of being sexually abused." Generally, you try to give those people you meet the impression that your life is perfect for fear of rejection. You want them to like you, or at least accept you and get to know you. So you put on a big smile and pretend that everything is fine. But what they don't know is that behind that smile is a horrible secret.

Victims of sexual abuse all have similar reasons for not sharing this information. It might be fear that someone will blame us, just as we blame ourselves. It may be that we don't want to hurt our caregivers by letting them know they trusted the wrong people with their own child—the most cherished part of a mother's life. Perhaps we just don't want to admit that it really happened because we want to forget and bury it. Or maybe we have blocked it from our memories in an attempt to live a "normal" life. Still, some don't tell because of fear that we will not be believed or because it is just too painful to bring ourselves to talk about. So we put on our masks, hide it beneath our physical shell and lock it up inside of us. Some of us are great at sugar-coating our attitude in the hopes that you would never guess. Others of us shut down and withdraw, while some try to self-medicate through drugs, drinking, self-mutilation, and believe it or not, sex.

I have hidden behind my smile for over ten years now. I kept my secret for two years, until it was told for me. I doubt that I would have ever revealed my past. After that, I still pretended it never happened. I blamed myself and didn't want to deal with the pain of vocalizing what I wish would simply become a bad nightmare. Now, ten years after my abuse took place, I am finally ready to come to terms and tell my story.

The following pages are filled with my memories. Some are warm and fuzzy, while others may be hard for some people to read. To those of you who have been through sexual abuse of any sort, this book might trigger some bad memories for you.

This is a true account of the first eighteen years of my life. I hope that reading my story will bring many to understand what it is like to be sexually abused and to understand that the effects of sexual abuse do not end when the abuse stops. I want those of you who have been through similar experiences to know that you are not alone. You can get through the pain and fear that you have felt at the hands of your abuser. You can move beyond it and make something wonderful of your life if you deal with it. This is my story. It is not an attempt to lessen what you have been through; it is simply to help you make sense of it.

As a young girl, I went through "hell" at the hands of two evil men, and while I will always have those experiences with me, I refuse to let them have power over me. I can't change what happened to me, but I can choose to use my experiences to show others how I dealt with it. It's also about letting you know you are not alone, that there are people out there who can help you move through it and overcome it. Thousands who have been through sexual abuse never speak out. They live with their secret forever; their stories go untold. This is the story that I hid—the story that has taken me years to finally be able to tell. I hope that other survivors will be able to do the same—to share their dreadful secret and begin to heal.

Love, Anita

THEY SAY IT IS NOT the destination that matters, but rather the journey. No one seems to tell us where life will lead us, or where it is supposed to lead us. We just have to hope that all the twists and turns and changes in direction will take us to where we are destined to be. Through the journey, both the smooth patches and rocky parts, we have nothing to go on but faith. There are no signs, no directions, and the no one gives us a map. We simply learn as we go.

While no one tells us the destination, we all know our starting line. The moment we take our first breath of life is like the gun going off to start the race. That moment for me was on January 17, 1989 at 5:35 p.m. at St. Mary's Regional

Hospital in Reno, Nevada. I was born to a woman named Katie who was twenty-eight, unmarried, and seemed unfit to take care of anyone else; she could barely take care of herself. Obviously, at the time I didn't know this. The man who contributed to my creation has no name on my birth certificate, and has had no place in my life.

If you met me today you would probably think I am an average 18 year old young woman. Recently graduated from high school, I was part of student government, president of the debate team, and was in several other organizations; I was a good student. I have the best friends a girl could ask for, and if it was up to me, most of my time would be spent with them. But after you get past my resume or asking me my favorite color or song, or what I want to be when I grow up, you learn my life has been anything but average.

I don't remember very much from the beginning of my journey. I have vague memories of those first few years. I know we moved a lot, but I am not sure why. Little did I know then that moving would become a common activity in my life for various reasons, over most of which I had no control.

One of my first recollections is when I was about four years old. I have a few pictures in my head before that, but it mostly begins at age four. I was with my great grandma, whom I called Mimi. She bought me a blue ballerina Barbie doll for Christmas. She had pretty blonde hair and blue eyes and I wanted to be a ballerina just like her. I also remember getting the movie "Beauty and the Beast" which I fell in love with, and I still know all the words to all the songs

ABOUT ANITA

when I watch it today. I loved my great grandmother, but I was extremely close to my great grandfather. He would give me tootsie rolls all the time and to this day, the taste of a tootsie roll brings back the sweetest memories of him and that time in my life. My voice was really high then, and those two things put together earned me the nick name "Tootsie Belle." I don't think I loved anyone more than I loved him (except maybe my giant panda bear, which was quite a bit larger than my tiny four-year-old body). I spent lots of time with him and my Mimi, and I don't remember mom being around much. Then one day my grandpa left, but he didn't come back. I remember asking for him, and they told me he went to buy a watch. I found out years later that he died. I still miss him.

Soon after his death, my mom and I moved to Las Vegas and I had one of the first baby sitters that I can remember. She lived in the same apartment building that we did and I spent the whole day with her and her boyfriend (or husband, not sure which he was). We went on a long walk to a swimming pool in the hot summer heat. It was one of those days where you could smell the heated asphalt the second you walked out the door. I had no sun screen on and was wearing a tank top. After spending hours in the sun, and being a red head with very fair skin, I was badly sunburned. In fact, I had third degree burns on my shoulders that produced huge blisters full of a clear liquid that I still remember as being very painful. As you can see, my mom's babysitter-picking-skills left much to be desired. This ability would be lacking more and more over the years.

{ 49 }

The next memory I have is of my mom and I in an apartment. I was playing with pink nail polish and she was reading a newspaper while we were singing to Whitney Houston's "I will always love you." I can't carry a tune, and I believe I know where that came from. It is one of the few good memories I have with my mother. There was another time very close to that time when my mom had a bracelet on that she took off and put on my ankle. I remember her saying how tiny I was, and that her wrist and my ankle were the same size. I think she really did love me at that point, or perhaps she at least cared about me.

Looking back now I wish I had that mom—the one who sang with me, noticed what size I was, a woman who spent time with me and really seemed to genuinely care about me.

Not long after that I was with a babysitter at the pool in our complex. She was tanning and I was "tick-tocking" around the pool (You know, when you systematically and slowly move one hand and then the other holding on to the edge of the pool). I had finally become brave enough to go around the deep end and was doing it for my third or fourth time when my hand slipped and I fell in. I remember frantically splashing around and trying to come up and scream, but every time I tried, water would flood into my mouth. I somehow got to the shallow end where I could touch and I remember being pulled out of the pool by some man who put me in a warm shower and just let me sit there. I was incredibly cold and shaking, and was so scared.

Soon after that my mom stopped leaving me with baby sitters and started bringing me with her. We stayed wherever it suited her. She would drink and smoke some, but it never seemed like an excessive thing to me. She slept with a lot of different men. I would get to tag along and sleep on the floor, or a couch if one was in the room. I know we spent a lot of time in one hotel called *The Plaza*. The men and rooms changed almost nightly. I don't know how long this went on, but I know that at one point I learned what a period was because of it. In a hotel room one morning, after a guy from the night before had left, mom had gotten up to take a shower. I was sitting on the bed watching television when I noticed blood on the bed. I asked my mom if she was okay and she told me that once a month big girls bleed, and that it is perfectly normal. It scared me after that whenever she called me a big girl, because I didn't want to bleed. When I got a cut or a scrape as a child I hated seeing my own blood, so I didn't want to do this in large amounts. This was the first time I didn't want to be like my mom, but definitely not the last.

Again we moved, this time to Texas to live with my grandmother whose name is Anna, and her second husband, Roger. I remember arriving on my fifth birthday and not being allowed to have chocolate cake because I wouldn't eat all of my dinner. While this may be my first memory with her, and not the most pleasant, all others were definitely an improvement. We stayed with them for a while and they were so hospitable to us. We always ate well, had a place to sleep and I remember it being a really fun time. My grandma would read to me, play with me and even taught me to tie my own shoes. I learned by attempting to tie her robe every morning. One day I got it, and I have been successfully performing the shoe tying task ever since. She was everything you imagine a grandma should be. She gave me lots of hugs and we had this little thing we used to say when we were leaving one another. One would say "See you later alligator" before they left, and the other would respond "After while, crocodile." Little did I know that the last time I said this I wouldn't see my grandma for almost ten years.

We moved again, to where I am not quite sure. Mom's drinking increased and she would go out almost every night to places with dim lighting that smelled of smoke and had lots of people. I was too young to go in with her, so she would take me along in the car and leave me in the backseat to sleep. She would tell me to keep the covers over my head and not to open the door if anyone told me to. It usually took me a while to fall asleep, but I would tell myself stories or cry myself to sleep. One night I was asleep in the car while she was inside doing whatever she did there. I got hot and kicked the covers off of me, and I guess someone saw me and called the cops, because I woke up to a policeman knocking on the window. Even though she had told me not to open the door for anyone, I knew policemen were good. He asked me questions about my mom such as what she looked like, her name, and I answered them the best I could. Then I had to go with him. For a while after that, I stayed with several different families in big houses. Some of them had other kids that I could play with. They bought me clothes and some toys, and while it was nice, I wanted my mommy. No one would tell me where she was. Eventually she came and got me, and I will never forget how nice it was to run into her arms. She hugged me tight and promised that we would never be apart again. That was when I still believed her empty promises. I trusted that she would never leave me again.

Soon we moved again, this time to California where I went to a new school. This was my second kindergarten class. There I got lice, which is not is a fun experience. I don't remember too much about being there except that my favorite part of the day was when we got to color. I especially liked the way the orange crayon looked when you pushed really hard. I still like the way it looks. The things that amuse us when we are kids are so simple and innocent. If only as we grow up we could continue those simple pleasures. Sadly, the way of the world and past experiences often keep us from that. Up to this point in my life I was able to enjoy those simple pleasures, but soon even simple pleasures would be taken away from me. I would be forced to grow up in a very unfavorable way.

From California we moved to a place for women and children in Nevada, and I remember riding on a big yellow bus that took me to and from school. After school I would go back to a center in a building made of red brick. We slept in a big room with a lot of bunk beds. My mom and I shared one, and she let me have the top, which at the time was so exciting to me. To this day, I still love sleeping on the top of a bunk bed, and even my bed at home is higher than most. There's something about being in a bed higher above the ground that makes me feel safe. While at the center I got the chicken pox, which I remember being a most uncomfortable ailment to say the least. It gives itching a whole new meaning. If you have been through it you know what I mean. I survived without scars and healed of the chicken pox. The time spent there wasn't that bad. There were lots of other kids there, we played basketball and I learned to ride a bike.

Of course we moved again, but this time to an apartment. I changed schools to Crestwood Elementary School and became best friends with a nice girl named Ashley. We spent a lot of time together. She was so nice and her hair was incredibly long because her mom had never cut it. It went all the way down past her butt. I would spend weeks at a time at her house and I loved every minute of it. We would play in the mud in her back yard, do finger painting and build forts in the room she and her brother shared. Her family was so nice to me, and I longed to be a part of something that nice.

My mother spent a lot of time going out, which I later found out was going to bars. Her drinking was increasing, but didn't seem out of control yet. However, as a first grader, I might not have been the best judge. She would usually leave me in our apartment or at Ashley's house, but occasionally she would take me with her and I would play in an arcade if there was one. Actually it was more like I pretended I was playing in the arcade. I actually didn't have money to put in the machines so I would move the joysticks and press the buttons and imagine I was playing a game. Of course, in my imagination I always won, but now I do not do well at video games and rarely win.

We no longer had a car so she couldn't leave me in that at least. One night I was in the apartment by myself watching TV when my mom called me. It was about seven at night. She said to get on our regular town bus and get off two stops up, across from the 7-11 store, and to go to the Blue Angel Motel. I did as I was told, even though I was scared to go alone. That night I met a man whom she called Dave. He was a little shorter than mom with short red hair, dressed in ragged jeans, a red flannel shirt, cowboy boots, and wore a mustache. I could tell mom had been drinking a bit. She said we were going to stay there for the night with him, which was odd to me because we hadn't stayed with a man for a while. Of course I didn't want to, but I did as I was told without any protesting. He was really nice to me and was really nice to my mom as well. We went to the room he was staying in and I went to sleep on the couch. When I woke up the next morning we all went to breakfast at a hotel restaurant called *The El Cortez*.

Dave became an active part of our lives. We began living with him and things were fine for quite a while. He owned an upholstery business on Freemont St., where he worked very hard. He used the money to help pay for apartments with us, and for our food. He was always very nice to me, and even called me his daughter. My mom always insisted I called him dad and back then I didn't mind. He was nice and said he loved me so he was what I thought a dad should be. I had never known my real dad so if this guy was willing to be my dad, who was I to complain. Mom even did better with him around. She drank and smoked some, but not as much. She actually had a job, and genuinely seemed happier.

We moved into a nicer apartment in a building called Maverick Apartments. We lived on the second floor across from some very nice people. There was a little boy who lived there, just about my age, who stayed there with his mother and grandmother. I used to play with him and another girl who lived with her dad named Heidi. I remember she had a ton of toys and while she was a bit bratty, I would put up with her disposition so I could hang out with her. Mom and Dave left me with various baby sitters, including the people that lived across the breezeway. They were notorious for picking me up hours later than arranged, and this didn't exactly go over well with the boy's mom. The lady explained to my mom that if she left me there later than she said again, that she was going to call the police for neglect. Of course, mom didn't listen to this. The next time they went out I was again sent across the way to stay while they had their fun. We played the game Sorry and I definitely kicked the boy's butt. (I am really competitive now, which wasn't any different when I was younger). The lady wasn't kidding with her threat, and when mom didn't come get me on time, she called the authorities. When they arrived, a policeman told me I had to come with him. I didn't want to be separated from my mom again so I tried to run. At six years old your legs can only carry you so fast and I didn't even make it out the front door. I remember being picked up kicking and screaming as I tried to get away, tears streaming down my face. I was so determined not to go with the policeman. My mom's story was she got hit in the head with a two by four, when in reality she and Dave were so drunk that they simply disregarded the previous warning. The cop overpowered me with no trouble and placed me in his car.

As we drove away I looked out the window through my tears at all the Christmas lights that decorated the surrounding area as we drove through. By this time it was getting late. We arrived at a building which housed lots of rooms with half glass walls and many computers. A lady sitting at a desk asked my name and I was so impressed that she could type without looking. She was a heavy set women with brown frizzy hair and a very inviting smile. She asked me questions about myself and then showed me a room just down the hall that had piles of toys inside where I watched Rudolph the Red Nosed Reindeer. After what seemed like eternity, the police officer came in and told me it was time to go. I gladly went with him thinking he might take me home, but instead he took me to a cozy place that looked like a cottage. It was well past bedtime so everyone else was asleep. I was shown to my bed and given clothes to sleep in.

The next morning I woke up and demanded to know where my mom was and when I was going to be able to leave. I discovered she had been taken to jail for neglect and I wouldn't see her for a while. I also learned that I was brought to a place where many other children lived as well. In my particular place there were only girls. I made friends with some of them; we played together and did various chores. I helped with anything I could and they always praised me for a job well done. Even at that age all I wanted to do was please others.

Since it was the holiday season, there were several parties the children were invited to attend. We received all kinds of presents and treats from people whom none of us had ever met. They were just people who were kind enough to share with us. Christmas was spent away from home, but I kept a cheerful attitude toward the situation as soon as they told me my mom was in jail. I hoped if perhaps I was a good girl I would get to go home sooner. It took me a long time to realize it wouldn't matter how good I was, nothing I did would change how she was.

On my final day there I was in the entertainment room and we were all watching Bambi. A woman came to me saying there was someone there to see me. She took me to an office where the moment I saw my mom I ran and jumped into her arms. Again she held me tight and told me she would never leave me. When I left they sent me home with all kinds of toys and games and candy in addition to all that I had received while being there. I was so happy to be home again. She and Dave were still together and we resumed life as it had been before. I went back to my school class and continued with learning to read, and I had to work on not calling out when the teacher asked a question. Both of these were a bit of trouble for me.

After a while things seemed back to normal. My mom didn't leave me with people nearly as much. In fact, she and Dave didn't go out much at all. I thought I finally had everything. The only thing I didn't like was when my mom and Dave would get into fights. They would physically hit each other, and I would just sit there yelling at them to stop. It didn't happen very often, maybe once every couple of months, but I still hated it.

ABOUT ANITA

At school things were going pretty good. I was still spending time with Ashley whenever I could since we had so much fun together. Things were going great until the time Valentine's Day was approaching. I was so excited for this holiday. We made valentine mail boxes in class on Friday and decorated them in red, white and pink with pictures of ourselves, so that on Monday our classmates could fill them with sweets and cards containing Be Mine's, conversation hearts, and chocolate kisses. I went home that weekend anticipating all of the fun. However, on that Sunday my mother called my grandfather in Florida whom I hadn't seen or heard from since I was two years old. I didn't think much of us calling him until she said the words that cut through my heart like a knife. "I don't want her anymore; come get her." I still remember that like it was yesterday. Was this how she showed love for me, especially at Valentines Day? I was crushed that my mommy was breaking her promise of us being together forever, without even so much as a care. I wondered if it was because I was bad or if I had done something to upset her. I didn't ask her why she did this; I just cried. Her father did as he was asked and got on a plane the next day to come get me. My mom took me to school the next morning to withdraw me, and I was allowed to go to my class for a few hours for one last time so I could pass out my valentines and collect them from my friends. I told them I was leaving and going to Florida, but I didn't tell them it was because my mom was giving me away.

My granddaddy arrived at the airport on a plane as he said, and my mom and I met him. I had a suitcase with some clothes in it and a broken heart. There was some time before we could get on the plane, so the three of us walked around the airport. I recall holding on to my mom's hand as tight as I could. I wasn't mad at her because I thought it was my fault. I just didn't understand what I had done. Being reluctant to let go of her, we exchanged one last hug and I got on the plane with him with tears filling my eyes as we headed for Palm Beach International Airport. After crying for quite a while I fell asleep, and woke up when my granddaddy offered me a snack. It was already light outside and the sun was shinning. Leaving the plane we were met by his second wife whom everyone called Mimon, and his wife's sister, whom I learned to call Nanny. I didn't know when I got off the plane that I was starting a whole new life.

We all climbed into the car, but I don't remember very much about that car ride. I remember staring out into the distance looking at this place that resembled very little to Nevada. Mimon and Nanny took me shopping; buying me all kinds of clothes and shoes. I also got a hair cut. By the end of the day I decided that living there wouldn't be that bad. Mimon and granddaddy had a huge house in Palm Beach Gardens. The ceilings were taller than ones I had ever seen and they had cats which I fell in love with immediately. Mimon and granddaddy enrolled me in the elementary school that was on the next street called Alamanda Elementary. I even had my own room which I kept immaculate in fear they might take it away.

Mimon and granddaddy helped me with reading and learning to tell time. They had me take a test to measure whether or not I was gifted. When I passed with flying colors they took my out to dinner to celebrate. Sometimes I got into trouble for talking back or for my lack of manners. No one had ever taught me things like that and there were so many things to remember in order to be proper. Everything was very proper with them. They had a lot of rules that I followed the best I could.

At school we each had a clothes pin with our name written on it, and it was on a behavior chart. There were three colors you could earn: green, yellow or red. Everyone started out with green each day, and if you misbehaved your clothes pin was moved from green to yellow. If you were really bad your pin was moved to red. One day my pin was moved to yellow and a note was sent home that had to be signed stating I had received a yellow light. I had already learned that granddaddy was more understanding with things like this than Mimon, so I asked him to sign it and not mention it to Mimon. However, my plan backfired when I took it back to school. The teacher didn't recognize the signature, so she called home about it. Mimon was angry that I kept it from her so she made me donate my beloved box of 96 crayons to my first grade class. I never got a yellow light again!

Other than that school went really well. I made a lot of friends and became really good with reading. I made respectable grades and my teacher was always nice to me. She would let me stay in from recess if I wanted so I could help her with classroom tasks. She would reward me with candy and I loved it because she gave me tootsie rolls.

Over time I met a lot of my grandparents' family who accepted me as one of their own. While I have lived with most of them at one point or another, it amazes me how giving and loving they have always been. I feel they were a blessing from above. I spent a lot of time with them, especially Mimon's widowed mother who lived just a few miles away, who also was very loving to me. She asked me to call her Mamaw just like all her grandchildren did. Mamaw had one of the most profound effects on my life because she showed me Jesus. Every Saturday night I would go to her house and spend the night and then on Sunday morning we would go to Lighthouse Baptist Church. Afterward we would either have fried chicken from Publix or we would go to Burger King and have Whoppers. She would talk to me about Christ and God and shared the story of salvation. It wasn't the first I had ever heard of this Higher Power, but it was the first time it was fully explained to me.

I was only there a few months until my grandparents decided they couldn't take care of me any longer. Mimon decided it was time for me to go back to Nevada. I didn't understand. Was I unwanted again? What had I done wrong? Was I really that bad a child that they didn't want me here anymore? They took me to the airport soon after school was out and sent me back to my mom. I was excited to see her again, but I was sad to be leaving all of these nice people. The next year would change my life forever.

The minute I got off the plane I was greeted by Dave and my mom. There were many hugs and kisses and I felt right back at home. They took me to the Circus that day where I won many stuffed animals, one of which I still have to this day. His name is Fluffy and he is a matted dirty stuffed dog. At one point he was white and his bow tie was a pretty pink color. However, now the pink is faded and he is most definitely no longer white. I won't allow anyone to wash him simply because I am afraid he might lose something if cleaned.

Being back at home with my mom was nice. For the summer we lived in the Bonanza Lodge on Freemont St. There was a boy about my age who lived a few rooms down and we used to play outside together. At the end of the line of apartments was a dry sandy patch of land that had nothing in it but a bunch of dirt. The boy and I used to find dead cockroaches around the motel and he would pick them up while I made crosses out of sticks and yarn. We held a funeral for each one giving them the respect we knew those who left the world were due. He taught me how to hold a football the correct way, and he played catch with me as well. This was the time I learned that I had no hand/eye coordination as far as playing sports, but I had fun. Sometime during that summer mom flew to Florida and drove back in a car that Mimon and granddaddy had bought for us. She also brought back a bike they had bought for me which I loved to ride in the parking lot of where we lived.

I really and truly loved that bike. It was pink that faded to purple and sparkled all over. It had a pretty white seat and white handle bars that had pink and purple streamers flowing out of the ends. I would ride as fast as my little legs could carry me. In fact, sometimes I would go too fast. I was speeding around the parking lot one day, seeing how fast I could go. There were places in the gravel that were wearing away. I didn't swerve over it fast enough and the bike tipped on its side with me still on it, taking a few seconds to slow down. When it finally stopped I had completely scrapped up the right side of my body, primarily my lower arm and leg. The pain was so intense, but the worst pain was as peroxide was poured over the wound. I can still hear myself screaming in agony as the chemical dealt with the bacteria and dirt that was embedded in my skin. Not too long after that my mom sat on my bike seat and broke it, so I never got a chance to ride it again. My beloved bike was broken and gone forever.

I began attending a new private school that Mimon and granddaddy paid for called First Good Shephard. The school was very nice and I had the sweetest teacher named Mrs. Fogerty. I used to ask her all kinds of questions about religion and she would give me children's books about things such as prayer and God. After school I would come home and lock myself in the apartment until mom or Dave would come home. This was usually late because they liked to go out to bars and places like that. When granddaddy and Mimon heard about this they paid for me to go to after school care, but my mom was usually late picking me up so the after school care said I couldn't come anymore. About this time, Dave and my mom became friends with a man who was about forty years old. His name was Jake. He was very nice to me and used to spend a lot of time around Dave's shop where my mom and I spent time on Saturdays.

One afternoon Jake thought it would be fun for us to go off together. He took me to his apartment and showed me around. He said he wanted to take a picture of me so being the fun loving six year-old I was, I put a sheet over my head and told him to take the picture. He said that wasn't the kind of picture he wanted. I asked what he did want. He then showed me a magazine with all kinds of men and women doing things that I had never seen anyone do. None of the people were wearing clothes! I said I didn't want to do this and he didn't push it. We ended up leaving his apartment.

After a while Jake convinced Dave and my mom to move into the same apartment complex he lived in because it was so close to my school. He also offered to baby-sit me when they would go out, for no charge. Sounding like a good deal to them, we moved onto the third floor and Jake became my full time babysitter. We lived in a one room apartment that had a bathroom and a small walk-in closet. This closet became my room. They put a mattress on the floor and I had a tape player that sat on top a card board box. I would listen to storybook tapes every night to fall asleep, stories such as the *Velveteen Rabbit* and *Mary Poppins*. I cherished those story tapes because they talked about how dreams can come true. I had dreams and was waiting for them to happen. Everything was supposedly perfect as far as the adults were concerned. We had a nicer place, it was close to my school, and they had a free full time baby-sitter.

I don't know if this sounds odd for a forty year old man to watch a little girl in his spare time to you, but my mom and Dave didn't seem to make the connection. Jake was very nice to me. He would buy me toys and clothes, and spent a lot of time listening to what I had to say. He told me I could trust him and at the time I believed him.

Things then started to change between us. I don't remember when or how it started but he began to touch me in inappropriate ways. He was also very interested in taking pictures of me dressing up, putting make up on me and posing me so some of my private parts would be exposed and captured on film. Looking back I don't know why he picked me. I wasn't an early developer or anything of that sort. In fact, I didn't finally go through puberty until I was well into high school.

I can recall exactly how his apartment looked and what it was like to be inside. When you walked in there was a couch on the right wall and a coffee table with a television stand right in front of you. There was an entry to the left which held a table for two and a small kitchen. Either way you went led you to his bedroom and adjacent bathroom. His sheets had sunsets on them and his room contained a nightstand, a dresser, and a big bed.

After a while, he was no longer satisfied with simple fondling of my body. He started to force me to do things to him, which were unpleasant to me. When I would cry, he would yell at me, telling me that he did so much for me so this was the least I could do for him. Being eager to please, and doing whatever I could to stop from getting yelled at, I did as he requested. I guess I have blanked out the actual first time experience because the next thing I remember is his hand pushing my head down and a bitter taste flooding my mouth. I ran to the bathroom to spit it out and rinsed out my mouth as tears streamed down my face. I was praying it was a one time thing, but unfortunately it was not

Again and again this occurred, with each time him wanting to try something new. One time he told me I would have big breasts if I would just swallow the semen, but that still didn't convince me to do it.

The point was reached in which I was spending so much time with him that I would even go there in the morning before school. He would fix me breakfast and at times would attempt to perform his usual course of action with me. He would attempt different things with me but I often cried, so perhaps out of frustration or perhaps out of fear that someone would hear me, he would stop. I question myself even to this day. I wonder what I was thinking at the time. I recall wanting it to stop yet feeling so numb and out of tune with the world. I actually felt I was an object.

Other mornings he would have me watch pornographic movies in foreign languages that had the English translations printed across the bottom of the screen. I remember the images being on the screen but I can't remember anything after he turned it on. My mom had apparently asked him to help me with reading and I recall him joking about this being an extra special literature lesson. This occurred quite regularly since I saw him almost every day.

Things at home were not much better. I was home alone when I wasn't with Jake. I recall one night being home when Dave and mom came home. They were seriously intoxicated and were taking off their clothes right in front of me. My mom made me watch her and Dave. I didn't want to watch and tried to walk away, but Dave came up behind me and stripped me of my clothes. He picked me up with one hand behind my back and one arm beneath my knees, and he clasped his hands together so no matter how hard I struggled to get out of this hold, I couldn't. I cried and screamed for him to let me go and finally my mom told him to let go of me, which he did. I was so afraid to fall asleep that night in fear Dave would start doing what Jake did to me. Nothing happened that night.

Things got better around home for a while but Jake was still doing unspeakable things to my innocent body and there was nothing I could do to stop him. I didn't tell anyone because part of me didn't think they would believe me and part of me was afraid they would blame me. Also, Jake gave me attention that no one else was giving me at that time. He would care for me when I was sick and would surprise me with gifts. On my seventh birthday he bought me the 1996 gymnastics Barbie doll that I had wanted for quite a while. It makes me sick now for enjoying any of the time that I spent with him. I hated what he did to me, but I longed to be wanted and I thought this is what had to happen for me to be loved. I wish I would have told my mom the night she asked me if anything like this was going on. I was curious about sexuality I guess, now that it had been awakened to me, and I asked lots of questions. She then asked me if Jake was doing anything to me sexually, and I said no.

I don't know if she or Dave knew what Jake was doing, but I do know that one day Dave decided this was a good idea for him as well. My mom was out and he began fondling me. I asked him to stop but he continued, talking about how much I should like it. I had learned from Jake that trying to get away wasn't going to work, so I simply laid there motionless just as I did numerous times with Jake. Dave decided to try other things. However, after no success, and with the threat of my mom possibly walking into our one room apartment at any time, he stopped the activity. That was the end of it for that day.

I still spent some time with Ashley. I remember one of the last times we were together her mother was sitting by me outside on a tire swing. She asked me if Dave ever touched me inappropriately and I said "No." She asked again and I started to cry, and the final time she asked I said "Yes." I don't remember ever seeing Ashley or her mother again. Telling her did nothing to help me. The abuse continued long after that day.

I was so confused. I wondered if these things were activities I would have to participate in if I ever wanted someone to love me. I hoped this was not the case. I wanted it to stop so much. It made me feel horrible about myself. I hated that I had this horrible secret to hide, but I didn't know what I could do about any of it.

Things with Dave didn't happen very often, however, Jake's abuse was almost a daily occurrence. For years afterward I blamed this solely on myself and when others would tell me it wasn't my fault, I would pretend to agree with them. In reality though, I just figured they didn't understand or maybe they just didn't want to believe I could have allowed it.

One memory in particular made me feel it was my fault. My mom and Dave had been gone all day. They had left around ten in the morning and I didn't see or hear from either of them until around five in the afternoon. My mom had come home for a few minutes and when she walked in the door I ran to give her a hug. I guess my mom was aggravated about something because she kicked me in the chest, which pushed me backward onto the bed. I just sat there in awe. No matter how things had been between us she had never been violent like this toward me until now. My mom left saying she and Dave would be back later. Hours passed, and it got really dark outside. I was scared being in this apartment by myself for so long, so I called Jake. He only lived two floors down from us so he told me to walk down the stairs and he would wait at the bottom for me. I ran down the stairs in fear, straight into my abusers arms. I know this sounds very twisted, but while he was hurting me he also had gained my trust. I guess at the time I knew what he was doing to me was very wrong but I wanted to be loved, and he showed me that he cared about me. It was as if I was dependent on him for attention, and in return he would misuse my trust and willingness to please.

We went to his apartment and he took me into his room. I knew what was going to happen and a big part of me wished I would have stayed upstairs alone. He began to kiss me but I pulled away. I wanted him to stop but I didn't have what it takes to say it because, every time I had tried, he had yelled at me. He gave me a T-shirt of his to wear to bed, and I went and changed in the bathroom. I kept my underwear on and

ABOUT ANITA

uneasily slid into bed bundling the covers around my small body. He began fondling me and I began to cry. How could I have put myself here? Shortly there was a knock at the door. We raced to put our clothes back on as he answered it. It was my mother and Dave. They asked if I was there and he said yes. Both of them were very drunk so Jake suggested I stay there for the night while they went off, had there fun, and sobered up. Something in Dave snapped. He didn't like this idea, but Jake just told him to go. He then shut the door and locked it. I stood in the kitchen while my mom and Dave went to the window where I could see them trying to convince me to open the door. I just stood there shaking and crying. Finally Dave punched his hand through the window sending shards of glass everywhere. The rest is just a blur until the police arrived and a policeman took me off to the side to question me. It was again asked if Jake had done anything inappropriate to me, and again I denied it. I am not sure why, but I couldn't bring myself to say yes. I remember being afraid I would get into trouble for it.

After that I stopped going over to Jake's. I was supposed to have dinner with him the next night and he became angry when I didn't go. He used to plan things as if we were an adult couple going on a date. Soon after that he brought from his house all the things he had bought for me over the year. He almost looked sad that he knew it was over. It appeared he felt as if we were breaking up and he was giving me back my things. I don't remember ever seeing him again.

It felt as if Dave knew what happened because he seemed afraid to hug me. My mom told me I needed to love Dave because he was my dad and did a lot for me. At this point I hated men so much I didn't want anything to do with any of them. A few more times inappropriate things happened with Dave, but not too long after he began, he would end it. I finished out the school year and was excited for summer. It had been a long year that was emotionally draining for me. I had a constant fear inside me that I couldn't shake, and I would dream of the things that had happened and wake up trembling all over. I didn't realize it then, but what I thought had finally ended was now beginning something new—the road to healing. I had no idea what was in store for me over the next years. That year changed my whole life forever.

At the beginning of the summer I flew back to Florida and on the way I met a little girl on the plane named Christina. It was ironic because we were both going to see our grandfathers, and upon arrival, we found out we were cousins. Many members of the family went to Florida for a while, and I was able to see all the people I had become close to when I was there before.

We spent the summer water skiing, boating, swimming, playing, bike riding and having the time of our lives. However, when it was time for me to go back, Mamaw decided that at 86, she was ready to take me on full time. Mimon easily convinced my mom to let me stay, so I was in Florida again. This helped me because I knew I would not have to see Dave or Jake. I didn't tell anyone what had happened in my past. No one had any evidence about what I had endured so couldn't ask questions. That meant I didn't have to lie.

ABOUT ANITA

I started third grade at Eisenhower Elementary in the gifted program. My class was a second and third grade split because they didn't have enough qualified teachers to teach gifted classes. I made many new friends and found a best friend named Leah. I became involved in all types of sports such as golf and tennis, and I would spend hours at the library reading a multitude of books. It seemed that through reading, I could pretend I was the person in the story, whose problems seemed so small. I loved Beverly Cleary's Ramona books. I once again could enjoy the simple pleasures in life such as: wondering what was going to happen next on my favorite television shows, being challenged to learn my multiplication tables, or climbing trees with my friends. I never thought about the things that had haunted me just months before. Sometimes, I would still have nightmares, but for the most part I suppressed everything that had happened.

Not only did the kids like me but the teachers did as well. I was chosen to be in school productions and I was referred to as a teachers pet. I guess I was an impressive seven-year-old, because I knew exactly what I wanted to be. I didn't want to be the ballerina anymore, or anything else the average child would give as an answer when prompted with that kind of question. I would answer with confidence that I wanted be a neonatologist, and when asked what that was, I was prepared to tell them all about it. I also was going to church every Sunday and always knew the answers to the Sunday School teacher's questions.

Glasses adorned my face. A doctor thought this might help with my drifting eyes. I would be looking at you and could see you, however, it appeared to the other person that I was looking past them. I had gold glasses and purple ones, and in an odd way thought they were kind of cool. This was also the age where I accepted Jesus into my life. I was young, but I knew a lot about Christianity from going to church with my grandma. I made the choice to be baptized. I now knew Jesus had always been there. When I was a child I used to cry at night when my mom wasn't there. One time I found all these listings for churches in a phone book and I had heard a little about God on TV. I remember pretending that God was talking to me when I was crying. He was telling me to just close my eyes and fall asleep, and my mom would be there in the morning. She always was. Mamaw helped me accept Jesus. All the time I went to church I learned so much about a God who loves you no matter what and sent His son to die for you. He is a Being that knows all and sees all, yet loves you still. I wanted to be loved even though this Being knew what had happened to me, and God did. He filled a place in my life that no one else could, and I have kept this belief ever since. God does amazing things. That is something that would take me years to fully understand.

A simple phone call. That's what turned my life upside down again. It was from Mimon explaining that the Nevada police had called her saying they had pictures that gave confirmed evidence I was molested. I would need to go to Nevada for the trial and testify against my molester. I will never forget the terror that swept over me as Mamaw repeated the information that Mimon had just told her. I stopped breathing and froze right where I was standing. It took me a minute to remember how to move, breathe and even speak again. Then it all came out in one big choking sob. Remembering that terrifying moment today still brings tears to my eyes.

As it turned out, Jake had taken the pictures and placed them in a Tupperware container, storing them in the air vent of his apartment. For some reason, maintenance men were working with the vent and came upon the pictures. Appalled at what they saw, they turned them over to the police. Apparently some of my old school awards and items with my name on it were in the container with the pictures, so that enabled the police to go to my old school and find out how they could contact me. They called my grandma, whom I called Mamaw, and filled her in with what they knew.

Mamaw asked me to tell her what happened and how it started, but I developed the story according to what the police had shared. I didn't tell her anymore than the evidence had revealed. I never mentioned about Dave and what he had done. I didn't mention that I called him that night the window was broken nor did I share with her how much I hated reliving this horrible experience all over again. She had me tell it over and over again so she could coach me on the proper terms to use for what had happened to me, telling me how to tell my story. I sat there perfectly still as she asked questions while I was forced to give her information of these traumatic events that I had hidden so deep within myself.

I was taken to Las Vegas with Nanny and Mimon the week I was supposed to begin fourth grade. This meant I would have to testify and see my mother and my abuser. I was incredibly scared and upon getting off the plane I began shaking. The shaking finally stopped and we were shown to our hotel. Mimon felt it was substandard so had us moved to a more upscale place called the Golden Nugget.

I was required to go to an office and speak with a women assigned to the case. She asked me all kinds of questions once again and it took every fiber of my being to compose myself during this interrogation. Then they showed me the pictures. I had to look at the photos that captured the things that had been done to me. There were about eighty photographs in all. I sat there completely in a state of shock, having to relive those experiences. What surprised me was I didn't remember some of them. I'm not sure if I blocked them out at the time or suppressed the memories, but you can only imagine how triggering all of this was as I looked at the pictures over and over while questions were thrown at me. After the interrogation, we went to the courtroom and I was shown the witness stand. They had me sit where I would be sitting the next day so I could feel what it would be like, and proceeded to tell me that I was to tell what happened, the whole truth. I couldn't stop shaking and crying as I thought about what I would have to do. My thoughts were full of anger toward this man for what he had done to me and for what I was now having to go through. At that moment, I wanted to escape the scene and wished he was dead.

A feeling of shame swept over me. I was so scared that I would be hurt again by the man who abused me if I told what he did in front of him. Terror overwhelmed me as I thought of sitting on that courtroom witness chair. I had been taught about Christianity and I had come to believe in God. That night I prayed that I wouldn't have to testify. I just kept asking God over and over in my head, "Please don't make me have to tell what happened in front of Jake and all those people. Please God." The next day I was still praying to be spared of this terrifying ordeal, yet everyone around me was saying I would have to go to the court room and tell my whole story. About an hour before I was to go down to the court room I began getting ready, took a shower, feeling the inevitable was about to happen. When I came out from the bathroom all dressed and ready to go, my grandparents told me my abuser had taken a plea bargain. Apparently, the attorneys had been trying to convince him to do this for some time, and that morning he went to his lawyer and said he would take the plea bargain. I definitely believe God had something to do with that!

After what seemed like eternity, we were finally on a plane heading back to what was now my home. I began fourth grade and told everyone I was on vacation in Tennessee the previous week. No one knew what happened or the ordeal I went through. I pretended nothing happened. But now I couldn't escape everything that had happened. It was out in the open and I was so ashamed. I felt so dirty now that everyone knew, and it certainly didn't help that some of my family members made up degrading nick names for me, indicating it was my fault. They never would say these nick names to my face; they would say it to others behind my back and those individuals would tell me about it. It hurt so much to know that they felt I was as worthless as I felt. It was as if they put reality to my shame and the feelings of inadequacy I already felt. I dislike that I allowed them to affect me.

Fourth grade was a good year for me. I had so many friends and spent time with them, particularly Lily, as much as I could. I was interested in the music group Hanson, whose concert I attended. I loved art so took many classes that developed my artistic skills. Softball gave me some more friends during fourth and fifth grade, along with a little bit more hand-eye coordination, but also a few injuries. During those two short seasons I somehow managed to have a ball hit my right pinky when it was pitched to me as I was batting. This eventually caused the nail to fall off. Later on a ball hit my right ankle in a freak accident and a piece of bone chipped off of the side. As a result I had to wear a cast and maneuver on crutches for a while. Consequently, that ended my softball career.

Due to my drifting eyes, referred to as strabismus, I had eye surgery in fifth grade to correct this problem. However, something happened with the muscles and I ended up being cross eyed after the surgery. That meant another surgery in sixth grade to correct the new problem.

Elementary school was full of memories, many of them good. But I did have the usual petty problems of someone not liking me or choosing sides against me in childhood wars. However, they were minor compared to the deep pain of my past that lurked inside of me. Anger was surfacing from me, not only toward Dave and Jake, but also toward my mother. My early years had been spent trusting her empty promises. So many times there were phone calls that promised Christmas and birthday presents that always seemed to get lost in the mail, and I was sick of it. And I was tired of her phone calls with another wacky story about things that weren't happening in her life or complaints of Dave hitting her when she could have left. This was her choice not to leave him because, as she told me many times, she loved him more than life itself. I guess I always wished that she could or would love me that much. I wish she loved me enough to want me, or at least want to take care of me.

Mothers are supposed to be the one person in the world you can talk to about anything and they will still love you. They know your faults and love you in spite of them. Aren't mothers to be there to teach you life lessons and hold you when you are upset and crying? As a child gets older, especially during the teenage years, moms and children sometimes fuss with each other and don't see eye to eye. But from what I've seen in life, once you are on your own, you and mom become friends. That didn't work for me, and many times I felt a great deal of anger inside because I couldn't have this. The one person who should have always been there for me, was the one person who was never there. I am her daughter. She gave life to me. Shouldn't she care about me, love me, keep her promises, and be there for me? That wasn't the way it was in my life. Perhaps she did love me in her heart, a least a little bit, but it wasn't evident in her actions. She didn't keep her promises and wasn't there when I needed her. She didn't hold me when I had a bad day, or listen to my thoughts. She didn't put band-aids on my skinned knees nor hug me when my heart was broken. I do remember when I was really little she would sing to me the song, "You are my sunshine." As I got older I noticed that the last line of that song was, "Oh please, don't take my sunshine away." It always amazed me that perhaps she took that literally. I wasn't taken away, she gave me away. I guess she didn't need her sunshine any longer. Often I would cry because my mom didn't want me with her, but Mamaw would console me and give me the love my mom didn't give. Mamaw did love me very much and took such good care of me. For that I am so very grateful. Since most people didn't ask questions about why I didn't live with my mom, it made it easier to not think about my mom.

Fifth grade graduation came with a grand ceremony that everyone but my grandparents attended. They had moved to California at that time but later built a house in Tennessee. They helped Mamaw pay for the expenses incurred while I lived with her, however, I didn't talk to them very often anymore. It was off to middle school and I couldn't wait. I didn't know exactly what it would be like, but I did know I'd have more than one teacher with classes changing throughout the day. I couldn't wait.

Good grades came fairly easily, but one thing I developed, possibly due to my past, was the need to have perfect grades. I would cry if I got anything less that an A on anything, even if it was a simple worksheet. I wanted so badly to please that I put a ton of pressure on myself to be as perfect as I could possibly be. A lot of tears were shed over this, but in the end I always ended up with A's.

I worked hard in school and over time I learned that I didn't have to have absolutely perfect grades. I still did well, and I got through the rest of elementary school and middle school with honors and awards. I was even accepted into the medical program at my local high school. I became involved in student government and debate, and I continued to make good grades. Throughout this whole time I still felt like something was missing. Other teenagers would say I had a great deal: boys liked me, I had many friends, I knew a lot of people, and I was heavily involved in school.

It was in the eleventh grade that I started to realize what was missing. It started when one of my medical teachers recommended a book called *When Rabbit Howls* by *The Troops of Trudi Chase*. It was about a woman whom had suffered sexual abuse and developed multiple personalities because of this. While I do not suffer from any disassociate identity disorders, I felt very weird when I read the parts about this woman's actual abuse. I mentioned the book and the subject matter to someone who knew about my circumstances, and they asked if it bothered me to read things like that. I said no because it helped me know I wasn't alone. I think that is when I began to realize that I had felt so alone in it all and I had held everything inside for years. I was tired of hiding it.

I began to feel a desire to share my story in order to help others. I started writing and noticed that I had very real flashbacks because of it. I began to realize how much my mom's drinking and neglect had bothered me. Somehow, I became aware of Alanon, which is an organization made up of people who are the family and close friends of alcoholics. The first meeting I went to was such an eye opener for me. I learned others had been through the same things I had. In the introduction at the beginning of the meeting there is a script that is read. One part of it, that personally spoke to me said *"Unlike others who will give you compassion and sympathy, we can give you something that few others can, and that is understanding."* I began to enjoy having this true understanding and by attending and listening to others I eventually was able to share things about myself. These were things I had never shared. Through all of this I learned about my strengths as well as my weaknesses. I can tell you that there is nothing more reassuring than having someone say to you "I have been through the same thing. Don't worry, it will get better." It's not the fact they are telling you that it will get better that is so significant, because anyone can just say that. It's that they have been through it and made it to the "recovered" side, and are saying that.

During all of this time of self discovery, learning, and sharing, God became a bigger part in my life once again. One of the things that Alanon taught me was to "Let go and let God." I began doing this when times got hard. I felt it was helping. I believe God takes care of me by guiding me. Some ask "Why doesn't God just guide us always?" A dear, sweet women in my group explained it so simply. She said "God is a gentleman. He doesn't step in until you invite Him."

I'm not going to say that the tough times have ended or that there are not more to come. One thing I have learned is "That which doesn't kill you, only makes you stronger." I believe every person has something that they are meant to accomplish. Something great. It may not earn you a Nobel prize or an academy award. However, some of the best accomplishments do not allow you any recognition at all. If it makes you genuinely happy, then that is your prize.

Eleanor Roosevelt once said "Never let anyone make you feel inferior without your consent." You have read my story which gave details about some of the most traumatic moments of my life. I no longer feel pain about anything that happened for I feel that it has helped me to become the strong, determined young woman I am today. If you have been through a challenge, whether similar to my circumstances or not, I encourage you to talk to someone about it. Holding it all inside hurts you. Also, remember that no matter what you have been through you can use it to accomplish great things. Remember to follow your heart, put your trust in God, and never hold anything back.

Epilogue

Anita has not lived with her mother since she was eight, in the second grade. They don't talk anymore and Anita hasn't seen her mom for a decade. Life moves on.

As an exceptional student with a drive that isn't equaled by many, Anita has many dreams. She recently graduated from Palm Beach Gardens High School where she was a Florida Association of Student Councils Parliamentarian, District V Treasurer of the Florida Association of Student Councils, Palm Beach Gardens High School Student Government Parliamentarian, a student minister for First Priority, and President of the Palm Beach Gardens High School Debate Team. As if that is not enough, she also writes for the Student Operated Press and volunteers in her community. Her other activities include working, babysitting, friends, and writing for a local paper.

Graduation presented her with three diplomas. Her first was for completing high school. She also received a diploma for First Responding—a person who acts on the scene of an accident or medical emergency, and another for completing the Pre-Med program. She is working hard to prepare for her college years.

August, 2007, has taken Anita into one of her dreams, that of going to FAU Honors College in Abacoa and studying biology in preparation for medical school. In addition, another dream is to one day open a safe place for women and children and possibly run for either the Florida Senate or Florida Governor. One goal she has is to write a *New York Times* best seller, a book of her own. Whatever vocation she puts her energy into must involve helping people in some beneficial way.

You can contact Anita at anitahelton@gmail.com.

3

Rick's Collection of Stories

Rick's Collection of Stories, written by Rick Beneteau

Dedicated to my beloved, and yes, this is her real name,
Jennifer Love.

※

THE ICE CREAM "COMB" STORY

SHE WAS THREE, JUST RELEASED from a far-away hospital after life threatening brain surgery, ready to take on the world again. I was happy just to have her back. My little "Mr. Clean" (shaven head and hoop earrings) and I were driving along to our local mall. It was hanging out with dad day.

I recall her words as if it were yesterday. "Daddy, can I get a treat?" She was understandably spoiled (if there is such a thing), so I replied, "Okay honey, but just *one*." Her eyes beamed like the sparklers on the Fourth of July in anticipation of that something that only she knew at the time.

We drove around to the new end of the mall on the normal seek-and-destroy mission of capturing a parking place. After all, it was Saturday. We landed a fair distance from our destination, and began walking hand-in-hand towards the entrance, her pace gaining momentum with each tiny step. A few feet from the doors she broke loose and ran hands-first into the thick wall of glass, trying with everything she had to swing the big doors open. No luck.

With a little assistance, she 'did it' and tried the very same thing at the second set of doors. It was then that I asked her what she wanted for her treat. Without hesitation, she matter-of-factly said "an ice-cream comb from the ice-cream store." Okay, the goal was set, and we were in the mall!

But hold on! What was this? At the end of what was just an ordinary looking lane of retail chain outlets she spied something new—a huge fountain with water shooting who knows how high into the air. The new goal line! She ran, and I walked (don't ya just hate it when parents let their kids run wild in public?), and we arrived at the spectacle at about the same time. The turbulent noise was almost deafening. "Daddy, can I make a wish, can I make a wish?" she screamed as she jumped with the kind of pure joy we've all long since forgotten. "Sure honey, but that will be *your treat* you know," I explained (gotta be firm with these kind of things). She agreed. I fumbled around in my pocket and pulled out what I thought was a dime (big spender) and placed it in her outstretched hand. She cupped it tightly, closed her eyes and grimaced, formulating her wish. I stared at that little scrunched-up face and said my own kind of prayer of thanks, feeling so blessed to still have this ball of energy in my life. And then like a shooting star, the coin was flung into the foaming water and with it, her wish.

We happily continued our stroll into the familiar section of the mall. An eerie silence ensued, which I was admittedly uncomfortable with. I couldn't resist breaking it. "Aren't you gonna tell daddy what you wished for?" She retorted "I wished I could get an ice-cream comb."

I just about lost it right then and there. I couldn't imagine what the shoppers thought of this lunatic laughing uncontrollably in the middle of a crowded mall. And needless to say, she got her wish, and two treats. Little did I know then that my beautiful little girl would soon embark on a long road of seizures, surgeries, special schools, medications and end up partially paralyzed on her right side? She never learned to ride a bike.

At seventeen, she could not use her right hand and walked with a noticeable limp. But she has overcome what life seemed to so cruelly inflict on her. She was teased a lot and always struggled in school, both socially and academically. But each year she showed improvement. She plans a career in early childhood education. With one year still remaining in high school, she and I, one night some years ago, mapped out all the courses she would need to take in community college. It was her idea. She volunteered weekly at a local hospital, on the children's floor. She baby-sat for our neighbor's children five days a week. On her own this year, she stood outside in line for four hours on a cold Canadian January afternoon and enrolled herself, with her own babysitting money, into two courses she felt she would need for college. You see, to her, failure was never an option.

It would almost be redundant for me to explain why I wanted to share this story with you. She *is* my daughter and I carry all those fatherly biases with me wherever I go. But these aside, she is a very exceptional person and one that I admire. I have learned so much from her. It is my sincerest hope that her story will have even a momentary positive impact on you as a human being, a parent, a spouse, or even, an entrepreneur.

I'd like to leave you with a closing thought. As human beings, we deserve all the treats, and the multitude of good things that life can offer us. We all have wishes and dreams, and the power to make them reality. Just simple truths of the universe. We can wish for, and receive, that ice-cream comb.

THE TINIEST OF GLADIATORS

I STARED INTO THE BIGGEST OF navy blue eyes and felt the power of his fighting spirit, despite the pain and week long raging fever. Most of the time my heart was in my throat and my mind was awash with counter-productive thoughts like, "Why him?" and "This isn't fair!" This wasn't helping him to fight (my daughter was much stronger than I), but in spite, he not only survived the arduous ordeal, but he emerged the victor!

I am talking about my infant grandson, Corbin Nicolas, clobbered with a serious infection of the lymph glands. This tiniest of gladiators toughed out what few adults could have, and not only amazed his wonderful pediatrician and hospital staff, but profoundly and positively impacted them I feel. My precious bundle of joy is not a superhuman little being. He is simply a child, like any other, who knows no different than to fight the fight and win!

I ask you, "What if *you* knew no other way than to just go out and win?" Well, that's how the true achievers of this world think twenty-four hours a day, seven days a week. Furthermore, it is the lack of this thinking process that is most often the sole difference between success and failure. When failure is perceived as a possibility, it will most likely become your reality. However, when we envision success as the only option, just as natural as gravity itself, success is achieved. Not without sacrifice. Not without setbacks. And certainly not without pain. But, it *is* achieved!

Personally, and most probably, I'm at least an entry-level workaholic with enough Virgo perfectionism to allow my thinking to stray off course at times. My stress level rises, my thinking patterns disintegrate and I become unfocused. Suddenly, my forward motion is slowed, halted or even reversed.

I was in such a tailspin when the call came from my daughter that something was terribly wrong with Corbin. Of course, business just didn't matter at that point, but it was through this trauma and "within" someone who has been on this planet at least 90 times less than me, and who knew no different than to "just do it!" that I found my way again.

Corbin was released from the hospital after his ten-day fight, better than new and all the stronger in both body and soul. I'm not a preachy person (most of the time anyway), but every now and then we all need a wake up call to remind us of the very simple laws that propel our universe. I received mine so close to home and in a circumstance that had absolutely nothing to do with the entrepreneurial spirit, but everything to do with the human spirit. I learned my lesson through the eyes of a child.

THE UNGIVEN GIFT

*H*E WAS PENCIL THIN AND walked with a limp. A thirteen year-old boy with huge yearning eyes who was always an unlucky patient on the children's floor of the hospital where my youngest daughter was all too often incarcerated. Curtis had sickle cell anemia, an incurable, painful and terminal disease that plagues young people of African descent. I would meander into his room to spend a little time with the rebellious loner and would often end up refereeing a screaming match between him and one of the nurses. The street-wise Curtis would usually win.

Over the course of a few years (the hospital was always my home-away-from-home), I eventually learned of the horror of his upbringing, the sad reality of his current life, and the apparent dimness of his future. My experience as a volunteer in a similar Big Brother program in our local Children's Aid Society, was that a small dose of interest and some one-on-one attention could go a long way to helping a kid who was in trouble with the law, failing school, and in Curtis' case, a social outcast.

So, when my time was over with the last boy I was involved with, I asked the CAS if I could hook up with Curtis, albeit 'unofficially' this time. Problem was, I was in the process of selling my dry-cleaning business while building a music production studio (for my next career), and my time was too much at a premium to commit to a structured arrangement. They agreed, and I began to hang with Curtis.

I learned in very short order that among his survival skills was the tendency to cajole, cleverly manipulate and even outright steal. Although always kind, I had to have a second set of eyes when in his presence and was forced at times to be, well, curt with Curt.

Also during this time, I was involved in a major lawsuit after having had a song of mine "lifted" by a one-time friend and co-writing partner in Los Angeles, who had become a 'hot' producer of major recording acts. On one of his multi-million selling records was the core of a song of mine he had heard and we discussed in my presence during one of my frequent music trips in the 1980's. I was a little more than hurt and felt I deserved not only the royalties for my creation, but also the credibility that went along with a "cut" of that magnitude by a name recording artist.

I retained a highly regarded entertainment attorney in Detroit (he represented many of the athletes on the professional sports teams in Detroit as well as one of the all time greatest boxers, and even some famous civil rights icons), who just happened to also be a truly wonderful and giving human being. It was in a meeting with this man that I casually mentioned Curtis and my desire to do something very special for him. You see, in my heart, I had a feeling Curtis would not live for too many more years. Sickle cell sufferers often died in their early twenties, or even before, a decade ago. I wasn't expecting anything from my lawyer in this regard, but the next day the phone rang and I was instructed to have Curtis "dressed up" and at the Palace of Auburn Hills at a specific gate number one hour prior to a Detroit Pistons game later that week.

He was a huge basketball fan. His hero of heroes was Isaiah Thomas, captain of the Motor City NBA Champs the prior two years. But I didn't let on to Curtis where we were going that night, just that we were hanging out. I asked his foster mother (and I use the term "mother" very lightly) to have him dressed nicely with his birth certificate in hand by a certain time.

Curtis was on time, eagerly waiting on his rickety porch when I pulled up. But to my utter dismay, he looked as disheveled as he always did in his over- baggy, tattered clothes. Of course, good ol' foster mom couldn't find his birth certificate. Now, can you imagine the fancy dancin' I had to do at U.S. Customs having this gangster-looking teenager with no identification trying to cross the border in my new BMW? Well, fate and some silver tongued talkin' prevailed and we were soon racing up I-75 to The Game. I tried to make idle conversation with the excited but slouching teenager. All Curtis could do was hound me. "Is it a ballgame? Is it a concert?" "Rick, where are we going?" he asked. I love to tease. Finally, he glimpsed the landmark dome of the arena from the freeway and knew he was going to get to see his favorite team play.

We found the specified gate, parked and walked to the entrance. Walking with Curtis was always a little frustrating for me (he would do the 'slow, cool stroll' and I am a brisk walker) but this time I knew there was something special awaiting that we should almost race to. We were met by a well-dressed, executive-looking middle-aged man, who just happened to be the Vice-President of Public Relations for the

Detroit Pistons. Talk about first class! He escorted Curtis not to his seat, but directly to the Pistons bench, where Curtis' eyes grew almost as big as the basketballs the giant athletes had just started tossing around in their pre-game warm-up.

I was led to our most prime of seats directly behind the bench. A waitress visited seconds after that, taking my order for refreshments. Everything was "on the house." I saw one of the assistant coaches introduce himself to Curtis, and next thing I know, well, guess who's center court tossing the ball around with his hero, Isaiah? Soon, he was running the court and shooting hoops with Bill Laimbeer, Dennis Rodman, Joe Dumars and the rest of the elite players!

I couldn't even imagine the exhilaration that this young man, who life never seemed to smile upon, was experiencing at this very moment! I mean, how could anyone's wildest imagination even envision this ravaged spirit and body trying to "deek the Bad Boys of basketball?" I just sat quietly in utter amazement, misty eyed and so grateful to my legal friend and the 'human' management of this professional sports team who arranged all of this for one person—a Canadian kid who was close to my heart.

When the warm-up was done, Curtis climbed up with me. The first half of the game was great. The Pistons were pounding their opponents. A few of the players even glanced back and motioned at their new teammate! By the time the half-time buzzer sounded, I was certain Curtis' dream day was complete.

But hold on, this was only half time! The same assistant coach who invited Curtis onto the hardwood floor pre-game, called for him to hang with the team in the sanctuary of the dressing room during their much-needed break. Give me a break! I'll never forget what I think was the widest smile I have ever seen as the team emerged onto the floor afterwards and my little guy 'cool strolling' as proudly as I've ever seen anyone, and much quicker than I ever recalled. What a night!

The ride home was quiet, opposite of the ride there. Curtis slept most of the long way home. I could only imagine his dreams. Canada Customs was kind and allowed him to sleep through their few brief questions for me. It was sad to see him sleepily stagger up the sidewalk to his stark reality, after having just left a world where I'd bet no one would believe he had been.

Somehow, I thought I would receive a phone call from Curtis the next day. But it never came. Two days later I had a very good reason to call him. My attorney and the team had arranged to have every player on the NBA Champion Detroit Pistons sign the game ball from that night, and Federal Express it to my home address, to give to Curtis. An autographed yearbook was included too.

I couldn't wait to tell him. I mean, I was flabbergasted at this unexpected and over-the-top gesture! I recall excitedly dialing his number and the deflation after hearing that "Curtis took off to Toronto yesterday." She went on to explain that she didn't know where he was or how to contact him. And neither did the Children's Aid Society.

Little did I know that evening would be the last time I would ever see Curtis. My instincts tell me that he is not with us anymore. But if he is, he has one great gift still waiting for him—The Ungiven Gift.

THE POWER OF SMALL

ROUTINELY, I RISE OUT OF bed before the birds, and watch the sunlight flood my office every morning. You see, I love this time of day! But what I don't love is being rudely rousted out of a deep sleep before my normal rise and shine time, yet every day for the past few months I have been.

I sleep with the windows open. At around 4:00 each and every morning, rain or shine, there has been this very obnoxious bird "somewhere" close by screeching his mating call at what seems like 130 decibels! Many times I've wearily peered out the window to be able to witness first hand what sounded like a pterodactyl-size creature on some kind of steroids. But never would this clever lil' creature reveal himself!

I appreciate nature as much as the next person, but this large sound at this wee hour of the morning is not music to my ears! In one agitated state my fine-feathered foe put me in, I thought about locating a 'sportsman' in the neighborhood to take him out, but that was only wishful fantasizing. Besides, I don't believe in 'the sport of hunting.' By now though, I had gotten pretty used to my tree dwelling alarm and looking on the positive side of this situation, could even thank him for the extra hour of work I am able to put in every day.

One day last week, I was pounding away on my laptop on the front porch swing, when lo and behold—*that piercing sound again*! And it was *near*! Imagine my surprise when after peeking out from under the canopy, perched on the telephone line above was this teeny weenie finch, smaller than my prized canary, warbling away what was really a beautiful anthem, at least heard at this normal hour of the day. Oh my, the power of small!

Now, may I ask, "How many times in your life have you thought that you were 'too small' to make a difference? How many times has this thought actually stopped you from doing something you knew in your heart was worthwhile?" Perhaps something like changing careers, starting a new business, creating your own product or even buying that dream home. Like me, I bet plenty of times!

Think about this. Every great achievement in this world had its roots as a single thought in the mind of a single human being. There's no exception. The greatest inventions, the biggest corporations, and the tallest skyscrapers were all borne of the single idea of one individual!

The difference between most of us and the Henry Fords and Bill Gates of this world is the total self-belief and conviction in their ideas to just "build it!" No matter the size, no matter the scope, no matter the naysayers around them, and knowing full well that the road to achieving their goal was going to be paved with major setbacks and failures. Here's one of my favorite quotes about achievers: "There are some people who live in a dream world, and there are some who face reality; and then there are those who turn one into the other."—Douglas Everett

You've heard many of the stories about the above 'icons' and people like Abraham Lincoln, Thomas Edison and Gandhi. Their journeys were filled with great adversity, devastating setbacks and yes, heartbreaking failures. But still, because of the sheer level of belief in themselves and what they set out to achieve, they were able to leave a legacy that today affects every one of us, every hour of every day.

There are millions of people who will never become household names, yet who have made magnificent differences in their lives and the lives of those around them. Take for instance, the single mother who was reluctantly forced onto the welfare rolls due to a deadbeat dad, and pounds the pavement until she lands a job, determined to excel, and works her way up the ladder until she ends up with a wonderful career to the benefit of herself and her family. Or, the foreign medical student whose family sacrificed their entire lives in order to send their child to a 'free country' to get an education, who, through sheer determination, graduates at the top of his class. However, he decides not to chase the almighty big bucks that await him in the 'land of promise', but instead returns to his homeland so that he may help alleviate the dire suffering of the people in his native land.

Or, how about the countless entrepreneurs who have taken a single idea and no matter what obstacles they faced, and the many sacrifices they had to make, created successful businesses with products that impacted thousands or even millions of people? I am privileged to know so many individuals who have accomplished great things only because of the great belief they had in themselves and their ideas. As such, I firmly believe that every human being, no matter where they

{ 101 }

believe they are on this roller coaster ride we call life, *can* accomplish great things.

As strange as this may seem at this time, I can tell you with all the sincerity I possess, that this great universe of ours awaits your simple and sincere decision, so that it can begin to fill you with all the power you need to make your dream a reality. It's a matter of truly making that decision and then opening yourself up to receiving that invisible assistance. "The Creator has not given you a longing to do that which you have no ability to do."—Orison Swett Marden

Now back to my miniscule, winged friend. On cue, and still prior to daylight, he shakes me out of my peaceful slumber. He knows nothing else, no other way. He just cranks it up at enormous volume at nature's call, oblivious to the fact he is impacting me on a major scale by doing the only thing he was designed to do. This is how we all should be, don't you agree? Oh, the Power of Small!

THE BULGING RIGHT POCKET

*I*T WAS ONE OF THE worst periods of time in my life. Recently separated, I had just lost custody of my two daughters and was forced to vacate my newly-renovated home (with 3 days notice). That contained the well-equipped recording studio I had spent two years building prior to selling my dry-cleaning business (in order to build a long-desired music production company). Divorce—Canadian style!

Two years before, I discovered that a "friend," a music contact I had worked with and even spent time with in Hollywood a decade prior, had stolen a song that I and my music partner had written and presented to this budding writer/producer at that time. He had since become a major player in the music business and had lifted much of our song, placing it on the album of a multi-million selling female artist.

After much consideration and consultation with a prominent Detroit attorney, we decided to proceed with a lawsuit against this record producer. As these matters usually go, we had to retain high profile legal representation in California and also sue the 'innocents', in this case the recording artist, record company and publishing company, with the hope (at least mine) that they would bring pressure upon the sole guilty party to get a just settlement.

However, I was counter sued for over a million dollars and had to begin dealing with that ugly business. At the same time, while living with friends during this confusing, dark period of time, a call came from my California attorney. I was forced to confront the inevitable—a trip to Los Angeles for a legal hearing. I had neither the heart nor the will to follow through with this. Neither did I have the money for the flight and hotel as all my assets had been frozen by the divorce court at the time.

I recall, as if it were yesterday, how Doug somehow sensed my emotional turmoil and just matter-of-factly told me to pick up the airline ticket at the terminal and then invited me to stay with his family. This is where the real story begins.

Immediately after meeting Doug in person for the first time at the airport on a Friday afternoon, I felt unusually comfortable. The hearing was on Monday but he had no intention of discussing the case at all on the drive to his home.

Instead we talked about our families, friends, careers and hobbies. His was mountain climbing, and he has since scaled the tallest peaks on the continent!

He told me about how much his wife and daughter were looking forward to having me stay with them, and that he had planned get-togethers with some of his rather famous friends. You see, we had built a rather unique friendship over the phone during the time building up to this hearing, but I had no idea Doug would be going all out during our short visit.

I arrived at his beautiful home in the Hollywood Hills to the warm hugs of Doug's wonderful wife and cuter-than-cute little daughter. If you've ever visited someone's home for the very first time and immediately and truly felt right at home, well, this was one of those rare instances. *Mi casa es su casa.* All of us had a great amount of fun getting to know one another and, as promised, we had most enjoyable Friday and Saturday evenings with Doug's crazy but wonderful friends in the entertainment world. I was in my element.

Sunday night was sleepless however. Although I was very confident in Doug and his abilities (I'd love to be able to tell you who he has represented in the past but the terms of the ultimate settlement in this action prohibit me from sharing any details that would identify any of the parties involved), I was still very concerned about being in court with four sets of high-powered attorneys against, well, just Doug and myself. Rumor had it that the defendant's father, a very high profile attorney from a major U.S. city, was also flying in for the showdown.

On the drive to downtown LA on Monday morning, we finally began discussing the case. Doug had put my mind at as much ease as possible as we headed toward the magnificent skyline. If you've ever seen the skyscrapers of Los Angeles in person or in movies, you will surely remember the tall, white, rounded building in the center. Doug's office was near the top floor.

He didn't park anywhere near it however. He pulled into this pay-per-day lot in a less than fashionable neighborhood many blocks away. Strange, homeless people populated the streets. We started the long trek towards the ivory tower, but suddenly Doug stopped to speak to an old man with a wind-weathered face. He was crouched against a building, clutching a "mickey" of cheap "Thunderbird" wine in his dirty, gnarled hands. He simply asked this poor soul how he was doing and if he had anything to eat recently. The reply was incoherent and Doug just smiled and handed him two, one-dollar bills. We walked onward.

As he repeated this gesture along our long route, even walking half a block out of our way to greet and hand yet another homeless person a couple of bucks, I noticed Doug's right pocket was bulging with what could only be one dollar bills. I didn't ask him about this ritual, wondering if Doug did this two-buck thing every day. Finally, and as if in another world altogether, we entered this stunning building and were soon going over the infinite details of our case in his impressive office.

Suffice it to say, although this case was settled somewhat satisfactorily in the end run, this initial hearing did not go well. After the hearing, and while Doug was in chambers with the judge and principle lawyers trying to negotiate a fair settlement, the other participants, all on the other side (some came with an entourage) gathered in the hallway. I made my way to each one of them and offered my apologies for having to have them and their clients involved. They all accepted. Even the defendant's high-powered father was understanding and exceptionally cordial. We started chatting about sports and he even made some off-the-record remarks about his arrogant offspring.

While this conversation was taking place, a loud voice angrily bounced off the marble walls, "So dad, you switching sides now?" My former musical friend was now in the hall, obviously witnessing his dad and myself acting civilly. I walked over and with a simple gesture of peace, offered my hand to him. It was readily and violently slapped away. I am what I feel most would say, a peace-loving, passive human being. But having the physical sting of an assault like this brought the instinctual animal out in me, to defend, and I began to react accordingly. It was a good thing Dad, who rushed to the scene, ushered his son back into the courtroom.

Doug soon emerged with the bad news that anything approximating a fair settlement was not going to happen this day. That disappointed me, but didn't seem to surprise my esteemed lawyer, as he assured me that we would need to apply more pressure in due course. Not a nice business. After our "tough day at the office," Doug was soon digging back into his right pocket on our way back to the parking lot, even placing currency into the hands of some of the same indigents. I then came to the conclusion that they weren't all strangers.

We pulled in to get some gas just around the corner from the parking lot and were standing at the pumps when a disheveled fellow approached us. This time it was me who engaged him in conversation. He was a Vietnam veteran with a severe chip on his shoulder and he seemed to be glad just to have someone to listen. As if by magic, penniless me turned to Doug, who, with a big smile had his arm outstretched with two dollar bills just dangling for me to take.

My thoughts immediately ran back to several months before when I encountered a homeless man begging on the downtown Detroit Street that led to the tunnel to Canada when I was returning home from a meeting with my Michigan attorney. I had a few U.S. dollars in my pocket and handed them to this man, but, with the following, loudly spoken condition: "This is for food, not booze!" This was not the way Doug gave. He gave as giving should always be, without condition. So, into the hand of this man went my two bucks along with my most sincere wish—"Good Luck!" He hobbled away, mumbling to himself.

Doug and I have remained friends over the years. We exchange email and he sends me a Christmas card every year as well as his articles that have been published in the top law journals. His giving though, went well beyond helping those souls on the street.

In the end, and with the final decision left totally to me, we made a settlement agreement that would not even come close to compensating me and my music partner for having created a song that was a vital part of such a successful, worldwide recording project, nor Doug, for all his time, effort and expertise in trying to get justice for me and my music partner. In Doug's heart-of-hearts, he knew it would simply end the great stress that this case represented for me at this totally tumultuous period of time. That was good enough for him.

I've never made mention to Doug of our long walk to and from the office in all this time but I fully suspect he still leaves home each day with a pocketful of one dollar bills, parks far from his office so that he can bring a little joy into the lives of the less fortunate, and, takes on clients that are in the same position as I was a decade ago. In other words Giving—as Giving should always be.

IF ONLY . . .

SHE WAS ABOUT 30 YEARS old; a pretty woman to me. She had several lines of deep scars on her face that I assumed were the result of severe injuries caused by a car accident, or worse, an attack. This disturbed me.

I noticed her from my balcony within days of moving into my high-rise, walking two little white dogs around the block. She was always alone, always with a look of deep sadness on her face. I must have run into her at least twenty times during my year-and-a-quarter of living here, on the elevator or on the grounds of our building, each time trying to engage her in conversation—about the weather, her dogs, anything to get her to at least smile. Never once did she smile though, or answer me with more than a couple of words. After each attempt, I just left her with my smile, and let it go.

Rick's Collection of Stories

Like you I'm sure, I have been face-to-face with people that have been deeply depressed. In my heart of hearts, I knew she was. Without knowing anything about her, I could only surmise that whatever had happened in her life to cause this disfigurement was the reason. Perhaps shallow of me, but I couldn't even imagine looking in the mirror each day to see such hideous physical devastation.

On Monday of last week, I proceeded out the main doors of my building to go on my morning walk. I noticed 2 police cars and a forensics van in the visitor's parking lot. My mind began to wonder as to what this could possibly have been about. I concluded that perhaps an elderly tenant had passed away, and promptly forgot about it. On the following Friday, I discovered the truth. I saw one of the building managers who had just returned from a funeral. It was the funeral of this young woman. She had done what was unperceivable to me—she took her own life. I was shaken. I learned in that conversation that her scars were the result of surgery, for cancer. I became deeply disturbed.

Truth is, I had thought so many times that I should invite this woman for a coffee, or for a walk in the sculpture park below our building, something where some friendly conversation could 'break the ice' and hopefully allow her to smile. Even just a single time. I have a gift in which I can make most people smile. In retrospect though, I can only now imagine that she had a great smile. But I will never know. Because, as many times as I thought to make this overture, never once did I act upon it. And being that I have been blessed to have been in a position many times in my life to have 'been there' for people who were depressed, and even suicidal, I again, *did not act upon it.* Guilty? Yes, I am.

Of course, I cannot afford to even begin to blame myself, a total stranger to her, for what she felt she ultimately had no choice but to do. On the other hand, I could have chosen to do something, and act upon my desire to at least try to help. The obvious questions arise. Would she have accepted my invitation to a coffee shop, or for a walk down the trail? If she did, could I have made even a small difference in her life and actually see her smile—at least once? One smile would have been wonderful to me. Or, could I have made even a small impact that would have ultimately led to, well, her deciding not to swallow the overdose of medicine that she did?

Thing is, I will never know, because I chose *not to act.* Too busy, of course. Too many other things going on in my personal life. Too many other things going on in the lives I was close to. Too busy in my business life. If I can take away one lesson with me from this dark experience, it is the one I wish to share with you—when your intuition tells you to do something not only once, but many times, *act upon it.* Your intuition is your biggest friend, whether you know it now or not.

It honestly hurts to know that I did nothing to follow up on my own intuition in this sad, sad case. It is even sadder to know that I never even knew the name of this pretty woman. I dislike, and try to hardly ever use, the word "if." It is usually used in context with a negative circumstance. In this case though, I can now only wonder would have happened, "If Only . . ."

THE GREAT WHITE YACHT

My intention was to write this article with a fairly clear idea of what I wanted to express. But you know what they say about intentions—at least good ones? I came out to my balcony with laptop in tow and started typing. However, the impressive powerboats and mammoth lake with ocean freighters passing by against the magnificent backdrop of the downtown Detroit skyline soon had my full attention. I chose to live here just because of this million dollar view, and I work out here in my 'second office' almost every day, so why would I be so distracted this particular time?

The answer didn't take long to appear. Coming into view a foot at a time was this sleek, bright white yacht with blackened-out windows. It slowly cruised by, as if to say "watch me!" She was indeed a thing of beauty, all 120 or so feet of her—the ultimate physical statement of success and achievement! Suddenly, my pre-conceived notion of how this article was going to unfold simply flew away, just like the flocks of roosting seagulls do as I approach them on my morning walk along the river's edge. I began to wonder exactly who owned this stunning ship and how he or she 'attracted' it into their life. No doubt the owner was taking several weeks off, or perhaps even the entire summer, to cruise the Great Lakes. Or even better, maybe this yacht set to sea in the Caribbean, headed up the Atlantic seaboard, entered the St. Lawrence Seaway, and sailed down through Lake Ontario and Lake Erie to pass by my balcony—to inspire me!

A lingering look through powerful binoculars made this ultimate status symbol all the more beautiful! I returned to reality, wondering who the owner could be. One thing I can assure you is that someone created a lot of wealth in order to be able to navigate this vessel past my building at this most appropriate time! You might be thinking that this came from inherited money and you could be right. The point remains, however, that one person, at one time, with a single idea, put into motion "the seed" that attracted all the money required to float this multi-million dollar ship down the Detroit River. Let's examine this.

For the sake of argument, let's assume that our "captain" here is also a captain in the entrepreneurial world. He or she owns, or is an integral part of a successful company or corporation. As is the case with most real success stories, this entrepreneur probably started with only "the seed" and a shoestring budget. The important question becomes, "How did this seed grow into the success it is today?"

Ninety-nine-point-nine percent of the answer most likely lies within the title of this article. They "thought" their way to the top! I can guarantee you that this entrepreneur "thinks" like the world's most successful entrepreneurs. He or she thinks "success thoughts." Are you wondering what success thoughts are? Success thoughts are simply those powerful thoughts you think, minute-to-minute, hour-by hour, day-to-day, every day, that set into motion the Universal Law of Attraction—what you think is what you get! Think success—achieve success. Henry Ford thought success thoughts. Thomas Edison thought success thoughts. Tony

Robbins and Donald Trump think success thoughts, each and every day, as often as they can!

As human beings, we are all subject to slacking off, and no person can honestly remain in a totally "positive mode" every second of every waking hour. However, the simple yet powerful rule is that your thoughts dictate what happens to you, not only in business, but also in your personal life. Think good thoughts, get good things in return. Think *great* thoughts, get *great* results! Change your belief system, change your results! Don't believe me?

Here's what Henry Ford had to say on the subject: "Whether you think you can or whether you think you can't, you're right!" Modern day master motivator Tony Robbins chimes in: "If you do what you've always done, you'll get what you've always gotten." (this *must* make sense to you). Famous author, Dr. Joyce Brothers, offers this pearl: "Success is a state of mind. If you want success, start thinking of yourself as a success." The Reverend Robert Schuller says: "The only place where your dream becomes impossible is in your own thinking." Donald Trump has it: "If you're going to be thinking, you may as well think big."

I wouldn't dare put myself into the same category as the above icons but I can tell you in no uncertain terms that *every* time I have reaped the financial benefits and personal satisfaction from having a project become successful, I *was* thinking the "right stuff!" Reflecting back on my entrepreneurial path, I can see that almost every time a project failed, I was not "in-tune" with the universe nor was I "thinking success thoughts." I was thinking limiting, negative thoughts, such as how much money I was spending developing the project or how much time was being spent to complete it. Or worse, I was visualizing it as a failure, which is exactly what it became! This is no coincidence. It's a Universal Law. Change your thinking—change your results! Even The Bible says, "As a man thinks in his heart, so is he." [Proverbs 23:7]

So, the burning question becomes: "Can *You* Think Your Way to the Top?" And here's the real answer. "Yes, You *Can* Think Your Way to the Top by thinking the very same success thoughts as the world's most successful entrepreneurs!" Let me leave you with the chorus lyrics of a song I co-wrote called "I Will" with the hope their words will begin to get you thinking the right stuff:

> I Will because I can,
> I'll Do cause I believe,
> The strength I need to make the change,
> Is deep inside of me.
> I'll Walk where I have crawled,
> I will Run 'til I can fly,
> My wings will fill my dreams will soar,
> The moment that I say I Will.
> Here's to seeing You at the Top!

THE HARDEST DAY

*I*T WAS ONE OF THE hardest days of my life. The weeks leading up to it became increasingly more difficult, and even a few days after, my heart is still heavy. Here's the full story . . .

Rick's Collection of Stories

My youngest daughter and I have shared a very special relationship for twenty three years. Not only did she have to face the normal day-to-day stuff of growing up in this complicated world, Teri was also given the challenge of conquering many serious medical issues and the accompanying adversity that comes with brain surgery and countless hospital incarcerations, rehabilitation programs, a never-ending merry-go-round of doctors, and the juggling of powerful medications to control her debilitating seizures. Then, as if all this was not enough, she was partially paralyzed on one side of her body and dealing with 'being different' from other children was also piled on her plate.

I can still feel the lump in my throat on her first day of kindergarten when she proudly stood at the front of the line that was formed when the school bell rang only to have this bigger boy push her back so he could take her place. There were many similar hurts throughout her younger years, but together we were always able to bounce back and forge ahead after a good daughter-daddy talk, and a refilled tank of self esteem.

Teri also experienced the trauma of her father and mother divorcing and her life being thrown into a state of upheaval. This is not an easy thing to get through for even the healthiest nine year-old. We had many heart wrenching exchanges where I did my fatherly best to reassure her that she was not responsible for mommy and daddy moving apart, and that we loved her and her sister more than ever. She lived with me for the majority of the time after the divorce.

Summer memories of Saturday mornings playing tee-ball with other handicapped kids and running the bases with her little leg brace are especially sweet to me. She learned how to sign at Easter Seal camp. An especially proud moment was when all alone on stage she signed the song, "The Wind Beneath My Wings," in front of the entire school body at her eighth grade end-of-year assembly.

The teenage Teri became increasingly more self-confident and self-assertive. She graduated from high school and signed up for college courses while volunteering at the hospital on the children's ward that had so often been her home away from home. I can still hear a sixteen-year-old's shaken voice and heavy sobs as I tried to help soothe a first broken heart. That day I think mine was breaking just as much!

Teri has made her father very proud turning so many tragedies into triumphs. Today, our bond continues to grow as other challenges and issues of life come and go. She often helps to guide me. There haven't been too many days that we haven't been on the phone, often more than once, chit chatting about something serious, or just nothing at all. That however, is about to change.

Two years ago she met Kyle in an Internet chat room. Yikes! They communicated online and by phone for months. He played drums in a Christian band and she really began to trust him. She eventually invited him to come and visit her in Windsor. Inasmuch as I suffer from the 'no one is good enough for my daughter' syndrome as much as the next dad, they certainly seemed perfectly suited for one another.

He moved down here a year ago and they made plans to be married later this year. In addition, they planned to move to the city where his parents live this spring, four hundred long miles away. The day I referred to in the opening sentence of this story was, of course, moving day.

I know from the powerful, emotional feelings that overwhelmed me for the weeks leading up to this day that the role of parenting never really ends. It became all the more clear to me that how much you love and deeply care for your children only grows with time. Something I wrote a few years back began to ring truer than ever: "Of all the good parents I know, I can't think of one who doesn't love their children more than they are loved back."

To be blatantly honest, I was very surprised at how difficult "letting go" really was for me because I am someone who believes himself to be at least somewhat plugged into the inner workings of this great universe. This was one of those goliath heart-over-mind struggles!

Now I must also fully let go and trust the universe that Teri is going to be okay and has made a good choice in moving forward in her life. I must live by my own promises to her that I would unconditionally support her in her choices and just send her positive thoughts and prayers. I must fully believe that as I have been allowed to learn and grow from every choice that I have made in my life, so must she!

A newer friend of mine, who just happened to appear in my life at the apex of my struggle, offered this to me the day before she moved away: "It's time to trust this fully and completely and ride it all the way through." So, I must make the final turn from my own selfish feelings of fear and loss, and make my reality that what has happened here is a wonderful opportunity for growth and advancement—for both father and daughter. Teri is walking her walk, and so must I!

I will always hold dear the bittersweet memory of the sunny spring day as she rolled away in a twenty-six foot moving van to start a new life far from her father's home, but never far from his heart. It will remain one of the hardest days of my life.

IS YOUR PAST PREVENTING YOUR PROSPEROUS FUTURE?

You'll never stand on the mountaintop unless you've stood in the valley.

WE ARE ALL 'WORKS IN progress'. No exceptions. We move from one point to another in our lives and hopefully in forward, upward motion. As night is to day, and heat to cold, we experience the very best, and the very worst that life has in store for us, the 'stuff' that defines our lives and forms our future. Some people are indeed blessed to have not experienced those earth shattering, traumatic events that rock the world for most of us. But more blessed are those of us who have, and who have learned, survived and grown from, such tragedies.

I write this for the latter group, those of us that have experienced traumatic events such as the death of a loved one, loss of a special relationship, devastating financial loss, or have come face to face with a major health issue. Probably, you have experienced more than just one of these at various points in your life. I know I certainly have. Please allow me to make a most powerful statement: *Our past is only memory.*

Memories become distorted over time. The original event, because we have re-run it countless times on the movie screen of our minds, will become colored—most often very brightly, over time. The more time that has passed, the more distorted the memory. The exact memory, or the original script if you will, will no longer resemble anything close to the original event. If a movie camera had captured the original event we would be very surprised, or most likely shocked, if we compared the real version to the current one we remember and believe to be our truth.

What is most sad though, is that most of us allow the ever-distorted memories we have to affect our reality today. And so often we find ourselves fearing the future based on the inaccurate memory of the past. This can be, if we allow it, very limiting to say the least.

A perfect example is someone who after experiencing failed relationship after failed relationship finally finds someone with whom they feel they can share their future. Suddenly, fears seep in and the person begins projecting the negative experiences of past relationships into the wonderful, untarnished one they now have. Before you know it, huge walls are being built and defenses that have no place in the relationship begin manifesting themselves. As a result, the relationship doesn't stand a chance to grow because the past has been allowed to permeate the present and sadly kill the future.

Another example is one that I have been a victim of more times than I'd care to admit. A new business opportunity or venture presents itself. The potential sounds wonderful and the excitement level builds. But it doesn't take very long before the fear factor starts finding its way into the psyche. Memories of past business failures creep in. The imagination starts running wild with all the negatives that "might" happen. Before the pen is even drawn to write the business plan every reason *not* to proceed further has marched to the forefront. The imaginary reasons for not moving ahead obliterate the sound, solid reasoning to simply "do it!" A quote of mine that is often used in print and Internet publications says, "The Greatest Wonders of the World we'll never know for they were destroyed before they were even built by the great enemy of man—Fear!"

On a recent trip, I decided to take the train and bring some books with me. One was given to me a few years ago as a birthday gift from a great friend, a very popular book called *Who Moved My Cheese?* You might have read this best-seller (I sure was a little late doing so). One of the characters, a 'little person' named Haw, ended up taking a long journey through The Maze that he and the other characters lived in, in search of 'Cheese' (symbolic for whatever in life you are searching for). The Cheese they had enjoyed for so long had somehow disappeared one day. Long story short, Haw leaves behind a series of picture messages for Hem to find when they decide to separate. Haw was to begin a journey of self-discovery through the Maze, and Hem was to remain behind holding fast to his old thinking that the Cheese was unfairly taken away and will somehow magically reappear. One of these messages was: "Enjoy Change! Savor The Adventure And Enjoy The Taste Of New Cheese!"

You've heard it said that change is the only constant in the universe. So very true. When we accept that as truth and begin to relish the challenge of a journey of change, we truly begin to "live life." Not always easy to do, especially after experiencing a major loss in life, but nevertheless, when we are confronted with the prospect of change, we should learn to accept it. Then we can embrace the new journey with a fresh, positive outlook.

I want to share an experience from my life with you, one in which I indeed embraced the challenge of change resulting in some pretty amazing things. For a short period of time I was convinced my life as a "creator" was over. I had sold a very successful dry-cleaning business in order to pursue my real passion in life, which was writing and producing music. I had begun to enjoy some real successes as a part-time songwriter in the 1980's and early 1990's, and the prospect of making my living doing what I loved most in this world seemed reachable. If I approached this move smartly using the business sense I had, I believed I simply could not fail.

After planning this major move and building a recording studio in my home two years prior to selling my business, I was not ready for what happened as soon as the proceeds of the sale of my business made it into my bank account—divorce. Before the studio was even broken in, my assets were seized by the court and I was forced to leave my home (I had custody of my children during this time) and studio.

I managed to make changes though and entered into a third party arrangement that allowed me to continue for a few more years. Although I was living the 'starving artist' lifestyle in the process and had managed to position a talented singer to have a great shot at "making it," it all came crashing down in late 1997. I was discouraged, even demoralized and very deeply in debt! My dream had evaporated and there I was, lost in The Maze.

That's when I happened to log on to the Internet for the first time and the possibility of New Cheese. It didn't take me long to come to the conclusion that I could somehow offer those online the equivalent of what I could musically with my business experience. A few partnerships were formed in tandem with my solo exploits and soon I was well on my way to what has evolved into a wonderful new career and opportunity to help a lot of people make positive changes in their lives. Savoring New Cheese indeed!

I can honestly tell you that if I didn't embrace this 'journey into the unknown' with an attitude of enthusiasm and conviction, choosing not to allow that devastating setback from my past to color my expectations, you certainly would not be reading this article. Change is inevitable. We cannot control so much of what life throws our way but we can control how we deal with the change. As difficult as it may seem at the time, believe me, we can choose our attitude and indeed prosper in many ways from our journey to discover New Cheese. Do yourself a great favor and take a few moments to answer this very important question.

RICK'S COLLECTION OF STORIES

THE PROBLEM MOVIE

"The other day I got out my can-opener and was opening a can of worms when I thought, what am I doing?"—Jack Handey

Problems; Problems; Everywhere we turn there are problems! The modern world and its monster media make darn sure you hear about problems. Every hour of the day, every day of the week, every week of the year there are bloody wars, suicide bombings, gruesome murders, killer storms. Throughout this non-stop bombardment of negative news we have our own problems to deal with: Money problems; Relationship problems; Health problems. Life is problematic!

Let me ask you this question. "Are you always worrying about your problems, dwelling on how bad things are and constantly thinking about the worst possible outcomes? Even if you're not wrapped up in your problems, do you still from time to time create what I call a Problem Movie?" You know, imagining the worst possible outcomes to your problem, letting them flash across the screen of your mind like your cable news channel? To a degree, I think we all do this.

One of the basic, immutable Laws that govern this amazing Universe is the Law of Attraction. I've written about this many times simply because I have been so profoundly impacted by it, in both positive and negative ways, in my five decades of living on the planet. James Allen (1864-1912), author of what most modern day self-development experts feel is the 'bible' of positive thinking, *As A Man Thinketh,* sums this law up most succinctly: A man is literally what he thinks.

Centuries before however, the Bible tells us, "As a man thinketh in his heart, so is he," (Proverbs 23:7)

So I ask this. If we know the Law of Attraction to be true, then why do we allow our problems and the negative thinking associated with them to invade our lives even a little bit, let alone dominate them as some people do? After all, no one controls our thoughts and thinking but us, right?

I don't profess to know the complete answer to that question. Nor do I know why so many of us seem to tune in to the bad news networks or read page after negative page of the daily newspaper. But I am learning more about human nature as I grow older. For instance, I have a small group of clients that use my Spirit Coaching services and a certain few individuals who have chosen me to help them confront and move forward, away from their problems. While most do exceptionally well because they are open to learning and applying what amounts to some pretty simple concepts, some I have not been able to help whatsoever. They seem to derive so much more benefit from being able to tell me (and others) about their long list of problems and how much they suffer from them than they ever would from finding a solution to, and eliminating them. I recall stating this very sad fact in a recent article, but I'll say it once more, these folks really do *love* their problems!

I see a similarly interesting phenomena with the new series of health related products I have helped to create. A small percentage of customers simply need to prove their theory that change is difficult. They do this by running their Problem Movies over and over and as a result they do not follow our program. They choose instead to remain steadfast to their misinformed belief, only to remain a smoker, overweight, or unhappy. Another failed attempt and yippee!—another problem created! These people will continue to own and grow their problems until they eventually learn that change does not have to be difficult. Some may never learn.

Okay, I'll admit that I feature Problem Movies a little too often in my own life. I catch myself writing the scripts and directing the scenes that I would never want to become my reality. What sane person would ever want what they're thinking most of the time to become their reality? Here's a very recent example of how I allowed the plot I created in my mind to turn into my reality.

I had no sooner written my last line of web and promotion copy to use for our Long Term Katrina Relief effort when I entertained the thought—what possibly could happen 'this time' to sabotage yet another noble effort by a lot of caring folks to help people. Yes, I went so far as to project the same kinds of obstacles that had been put into my path previously with such charity projects. In other words, what kind of villain was I going to cast in the movie I had just set into motion? Right, old fears rearing ugly faces! Wasn't a long thought but it surely was potent! We no longer had clicked send to launch this project to hundreds of influential and possible promotion partners and then to tens of thousands of potential donors, when we began to experience major server issues. Nobody could access our website! And this challenge went on for days.

But hold on, there's a sequel. Once these server issues were finally fixed we discovered another. Any links to the donation site would automatically and mysteriously "redirect" to the main business website of my partner, and originator of this project, jl Scott. Another technical snafu. No wonder we weren't getting any donations! I was by then working on other things, and jl was packing up to move north and out of the path of Hurricane Rita, so neither of us took notice right away.

In the normal scheme of things, when a link is broken, you will receive a polite email from someone letting you know of the problem. What happened next, I was not prepared for, but should have expected. Into my inbox came this rhetorical assault on the integrity of our Long Term Katrina Relief project, even calling it a scam! This subscriber of mine came loaded and "gunnin' for bear." As he attached this constitution-length document, full of untruths and venomous assertions that he threatened to blast all over the Internet via discussion boards and lists, including the sending of press releases if I personally didn't "fix" this. There was nothing to fix but a server glitch to get the website appearing again. This misguided soul must have put a lot of effort into making the movie that produced such an overture. I could only imagine how much good he could have done to help our cause with all the time and energy he spent trying to tear it down!

Needless to say, we took care of this incident quite quickly but simply stated, I was equally responsible for the receipt of that email as it was me who put those kinds of negative thoughts out there, projecting a fear-based outcome and setting into motion the very incident I just described. The Law of Attraction is indeed a very powerful force! I've always loved what Shakespeare had to say about thoughts: "Make not your thoughts your prisons." Have you too spent time in your life as a willing prisoner?

Back to our problems. We all have them and always will. I've often likened life to a roller coaster ride with its ups and downs and twists and turns and moments of boredom followed by moments of sheer terror. No matter where we are on that ride and what problems exist in our lives, we always have the choice of how and what we think. We are always the writer and director of our own movies. It goes without saying that burying your head in the sand and ignoring a problem will never solve it. But neither will creating and then running and rerunning a Problem Movie, fraught with fear-based outcomes that are self-fulfilling by universal decree. If the opening scenes of a Problem Movie start rolling on the screen of your mind, be quick to take a commercial break, change the reel and start another, one perhaps, where a solution has been found whether you have found it or not, or, one that doesn't star your problem at all! Remember, you control every thought you have, and every thought you have dictates your reality!

Anyone for popcorn and a good movie? Great, because you have my heartfelt wishes for a lifetime of Happy Endings!

Epilogue

Rick has worn many hats during his half century of living. Straight out of high school, he started working for his family drycleaning business, eventually managing it and finally purchasing the multi-store company from his father.

Throughout the 1970's and 1980's, while firing up the boilers at five a.m., six days a week, Rick pursued his true passion; writing, recording and pitching songs. He won Billboard Magazine's International Songwriting Competition the first two years running as well as other major music competitions at the time. Music publishers and recording companies started to pick up his material as well. Based upon this success, he sold his drycleaning business in the 1990's in order to form a music production company. He spent two years building a professional recording facility in his home. Unfortunately, the same month his production company was launched, his marriage ended, and his assets, including the studio and music royalties, were seized by the divorce court.

Devastated, and unwilling to lead the starving artist lifestyle, Rick made his way to the Internet and began using his entrepreneurial and creative skills to become one of the original Internet marketers. He created top-selling marketing products such as: Ezine Marketing Machine, Branding You and Breaking the Bank, and he originated the Internet's first two-tier affiliate program with his traveling billboards, I.D. IT! Plates.

Rick's articles and quotes have been featured in hundreds of Internet newsletters as well as in magazines and print books. One of his most popular quotations has it: Give a shelterless man tools and he will build a home. Inspire him, encourage him, give him vision, and he will build an empire.

In 2000, Rick founded the Internet's first toy drive, an online holiday mainstay for six years. Recruiting the top Internet marketers in large promotional campaigns aimed at making sure no child is left without at least one gift under the Christmas tree, InternetToyDrive.org is a corporate sponsor in direct affiliation with the official Toys for Tots program.

The tragic events of September 11, 2001 affected Rick so profoundly, that he decided to change direction from helping people build online businesses to simply helping build people. His breakthrough ebook from 2002, Success: a Spiritual Matter, the first in a series of products that bridge business success and spirituality, remains an entrepreneur's favorite to this day. In 2003, Rick's first print book, A Large Slice of Life to Go, Please! was published, landing him the prestigious Pinnacle Book Achievement Award and many high-level endorsements.

His current line of NLP products like Quit Smoking Right Now, Make Every Day A Great Day, and Better Sales Right Now, are licensed by some of the world's top self-development entities. Rick is again at the forefront of the Internet with his popular personal growth podcasts located at www.MentorAudio.com.

On the morning of July 15, 2006, he received two emails, one right after the other, that affected his life most profoundly. The first was a CNN Breaking News Alert outlining the latest gory details about the bloodbath in the Middle East. This particular email made him nauseous, literally. The next email was from a man Rick hardly knew, Julian Kalmar. Julian explained that he couldn't sleep that night, fearing for the lives of two dear friends, one in Lebanon and one in Israel, who were caught in the crossfire. He wrote that he had asked the Universe what he could do to help, and moments later the phrase: "10 Million Votes for Peace" jumped into his mind. That was Rick's cue to call Julian. At 6:42 a.m. they began to discuss what Rick refers to in jest, as the "battle plan for peace." The project eventually became known as 10 Million Clicks for Peace.

Rick has two beautiful daughters; Sara, about to celebrate her 30th birthday, and Teri, 25. He's the proudest grandfather of the "apples of his eye", Corbin, 7, and Cameron, 6. He resides in Brantford, Ontario with his love, Jennifer Love to be precise.

Rick's future plans include doing his part to tackle other global problems as well as hunkering down in a cozy little pad on a lake to begin writing music again, to bring joy, success and even more peace to people's lives.

You can contact Rick by email at rick@interniche.net (please put *Seven Roads to Glory* in the Subject) and visit 10 Million Clicks for Peace at www.tenmillionclicksforpeace.org.

4

Carolyn's Life Reflection

Carolyn's Life Reflection

*Dedicated to those individuals whose hearts are heavy,
who want to feel hope, and want to believe that
their life can become extraordinary.*

LIFE IS A FUNNY THING. We are born into a particular family, raised in a particular place, given certain guidelines and expectations to follow by the people in our life, and we travel the road that seems to be plotted for us, often without considering any other way. We accept the course given to us without a thought and simply travel it without realizing we have a choice. While it may not have been possible to change our initial earthly heritage, it is possible to change the course we now travel. This I learned on my journey after multiple decades, and my perception of life transformed from accepting what was given to me to knowing my inborn power to choose what I want for my life.

My life began in a small town in Southern New Jersey, home of those big brown-eyed Jersey cows. Like those cows, I was endowed with large brown eyes, so often I'm told my eyes look like cow eyes. Any connection I wonder? I had center stage until siblings arrived on the scene nine and thirteen years later. Life was very structured and rigid religious guidelines were employed. I had to adhere to more don'ts than do's, but accepted all as the way it had to be.

My teenage years created a new dilemma for me. I had questions and wondered deeply about things. My mind seemed to travel to places I didn't understand but because of the religious beliefs of my family I couldn't get satisfying answers. Neither did I feel I could share my innermost thoughts. Therefore, I buried them deep within me and created a rebellious attitude during that era of my life. My wings were spreading and wanted to fly, but they were continually clipped, making flying impossible at that time.

So, the stage was set for me at an early age to ignore my inner thoughts and follow what I was told to do. If I didn't, I would be punished, something I didn't like too much. Like it or not, it was difficult for me to follow the rules, so punishment loomed over me and a feeling of unworthiness and guilt permeated my innermost being just as an early morning fog filters upon the earth. College years came and much fear erupted. From my very sheltered upbringing, which included small church schools for my education, entering a major university kind of knocked me for a loop. My eyes were certainly opened to the ways of the world in a big way. I developed a spastic colon and other discomforts, all of which I learned later were simply from the stress of new things making waves but old patterns and beliefs causing major fear if I ventured into new territory. Not knowing this at that time, I continued the journey plotted for me in the best way I could.

Forced into taking piano lessons and hating it for years, yet finding I was proficient in learning the skill, I began accompanying for church and my school choruses, then finally became the college accompanist for many events in the university. Solo performing made me extremely nervous but accompanying seemed much easier. This was one of those things that proved to be better than it originally appeared to be. Not knowing what else to study in college, I had decided on music education and piano. After all, everyone needed to attend college and earn a degree or you couldn't amount to much, or so I was told. But this proved to be a valuable step on my journey since I ended up teaching piano lessons to hundreds of children and adults over a 32 year period, earning recognition for the proficiency of my students. This allowed me to remain at home (my piano studio was in my home) while I raised my five children.

Marriage and children were my biggest dream during my early years. Because it was my heart's desire, I manifested it into reality. My children—three daughters and two sons—are my greatest gifts in this world, and being a mother was even better than I dreamed it would be. Not that everything connected to motherhood had dream-like qualities, but the hearts and spirits of those children brought continual joy into my life. They are now grown, most with their own children, and they continue to be a highlight in my life.

But the marriage was a different story. The original idea of *marry-the-Prince-and-live-happily-ever-after* never synthesized into my reality. Plagued with arguing and frustration, even early on, I felt I was on a continuous roller coaster ride with sharp curves and fast falls, never knowing whether we'd make it to the end or not. We didn't. After 32 years I knew my spirit was dying. I had considered leaving many times, but I finally made the choice to end both of our misery. My youngest child was 16, one of the three still at home, but they were old enough to handle the change more easily. There would be no shuffling of them to and from different locations to live or visit.

For years I had been waiting for my husband to become what I wanted. I had expectations and I imagine so did he. I expected him to make me happy, but he never could. So as things surfaced in my life, whom do you think I blamed for their occurrence? We had tried counseling but communication was something we could never get a handle on. Yet, I had been brought up to believe that you keep trying and divorce is not really an option. Then there was the ever-present feeling that I would be failing if we ended the marriage. But one day, a small happening—kind of the straw that broke the camel's back—opened my eyes to see this was not good for anyone, and I couldn't imagine God wanting us to remain together because of some rule. Neither could I any longer believe God made such a rule, which I had been taught years earlier.

My children filled so much of my life and my piano teaching was certainly an important part, so I gave many extra hours to them. As an expert seamstress I sewed many of our clothes, cooked from scratch, was an avid gardener, stayed involved with my children's activities, spent time with them every evening, always welcomed their friends for meals and overnight visits, as well as doing many extras in the music world (accompanying soloists, church pianist, chairman of organizations, etc.). I loved this life except for one thing, I wasn't really happy. How could this be I'd wonder? I had so much of what I wanted except for a happy marriage, so naturally that is what I blamed for my unhappiness.

For many years I endured a multitude of physical symptoms for which doctors couldn't find a cause, so simply labeled them stress-related. I felt the stress was the roller coaster marriage, and although it certainly contributed a great deal to the stress, there were many other factors that I came to see in later years. Doctors offered solutions to my varied physical symptoms over the years—the band-aid approach of give a pill for the symptoms. Sometimes the symptoms would lessen or even disappear for a while, but a cure never happened. I was pushing and striving to feel good about myself, wanting to feel worthy yet still harboring much guilt. Of course I did not understand this at the time, but I did know I was unmistakably miserable. So I'd produce more clothes, get involved with another committee, or anything to stay busy, hoping this would allow me to feel better about myself. All the time I was in a continuous state of tearing down my health.

When my oldest daughter decided to get married and wanted me to design and create her wedding and gown, I was delighted. Talk about busy, and the end result was a beautiful gown on which 35,000 pearls and sequins were sewn one at a time by me. All the flowers (silk) I put together as well as all decorations for a total cost of $6,200.00—not bad for a beautiful, large wedding. Many accolades came my way and I relished in them for a time, but the feeling faded away soon and I was left with that hollow, empty, restless feeling of wanting something more, or more to the point—the relentless longing to produce something new to feel better about myself.

The bottled up feelings of unworthiness, guilt, shame and anger that had been swept under the rug of my soul continued to churn. It was as if I was a time bomb ready to blow, and one day I blew. Extremely anxious and restless, I visited my homeopathic doctor. After listening to my symptoms, he prescribed a homeopathic remedy he thought perfect for me. Little did I know that in that moment when I ingested that small amount of remedy, my life would change in a way I could have never imagined. It would be an explosive step that would begin my incredible journey to my personal transformation.

My body reacted severely to this remedy, a quite unusual reaction I was told. Some years later, I learned that some people, who have a high vibration, react more than others do. It was obvious I had a high vibration and because my physical symptoms were more extreme than normal, I resorted to using the medical profession's temporary help for relief. It was as though I had a breakdown in 24 hours—physical shaking, horrific anxiety, insomnia for days, elevated pulse rate, racing heart, colon issues, and many other symptoms. (Most people react slightly when they ingest a homeopathic remedy. It works at a deep emotional level as well as the physical level, so can become a little worse for a short time and then heals deeply, often for good.) It felt as if my world had come crashing down and I was out of control, a frightful way to feel. We were moving back to Atlanta, Georgia from Tallahassee, Florida, something I wanted to do, but my condition and the resulting anxiety made getting there more than difficult to handle. In a state of sheer panic, I accepted the medical profession's offer of a quick fix remedy, namely that of the anti-anxiety prescription drug Xanax.

During the next three years I frequented so any holistic practitioners seeking a cure for my condition, and wondering if I'd ever be okay again. I felt like a yoyo with one telling me one thing and another something different, and me trying it all. Desperately I tried every avenue I could in the alternative modalities of the physical realm. I chose this route because the medical profession had never helped me cure anything and I was drawn to alternative modalities for finding a solution. I think on some level I knew I'd finally be okay. I kept praying for healing, but while living in the middle of this challenge, I had many doubts. I didn't have the support of my family either, probably because they didn't understand what was happening to me. I didn't either. I really believe they thought I had flipped out, you know, gone completely bonkers.

It was during all of this turbulence my oldest son introduced the idea of our opening a health store. "Are you crazy?" was my initial thought. "How in the world could I handle the daily routine of operating a store when I can't function normally in my regular routine?" So, I fought the idea, yet deep inside I felt it was a good thing to do. A year after moving back to Atlanta, in spite of my illness, we opened our first store, though I had many doubts about my performance given my health condition. However, this health store ended up being a great gift for it brought a wealth of information right to my fingertips. I became an avid researcher and seeker of health knowledge. As customers came into our store looking for help, I helped them and myself at the same time as I searched for the answers.

I improved in some ways physically but still found it difficult on many days to function in the store. I vividly remember on many days driving to the store with tears rolling down my face as I prayed for enough energy to get through the day. More than once I felt so weak I laid down on the floor of the back room hoping no one would come in for a while so I could regain some strength. I had often done this at home—literally laid down on my floor in whatever room I was in to regain enough energy to continue with whatever I had been doing. It was an agonizing way to live and I was always concerned about not being able to be there enough for my children who were still at home. Pushing through my daily routine seemed like an unbearable chore much of the time and I went nowhere alone for fear of anxiety attacks or not having enough energy. When someone was with me I seemed to manage a bit better. The panic attacks still continued.

A breakthrough finally came after more than three years of agony when I became aware of the emotional component for healing through some books that suddenly appeared one day, books like *Heal Your Body* by Louise Hay and later *Feelings Buried Alive Never Die* by Karol Truman. I learned I was holding onto a vast array of negative patterns—anger, shame, guilt, and worthlessness—and according to the information I was reading, they were keeping me from physical wholeness. The pivotal moment came when I realized that I had to forgive myself first, then those I perceived had hurt me. The only person who was suffering was me because the people I blamed for these negative emotions weren't bothered by them at all. That was the most amazing thing to me—I was the creator of my own stress and illness. However, as you can well imagine, it wasn't easy to forgive at first. In my mind my negative feelings were justified. Nevertheless, within a few short weeks of beginning the forgiveness process, my health improved significantly and I was feeling like a new person. Although it took additional months to heal, for the first time in many years I began to feel like my future was indeed bright.

Like an explosion of fireworks, a light turned on in my mind as I understood a most significant fact of life—I am the creator of my life experiences. As a creation of the Creator of the universe, I have the inborn power to create my life the way I want it. It simply depends on my thoughts. This was a totally new concept for me. I now understood about the energetic force from which everything in the universe is made, and the vibrations sent out from my energy or any energy are either going to be positive or negative. The positive vibrations expand into more good whereas negative emotions—guilt, shame, hurt, anger, lack of forgiveness, low self-worth—expand into more of the same. Wherever you focus, that's what shows up in your life. I realized for the first time in my life that everything I had experienced and was currently experiencing was a gift, and that I had the power to turn it into something positive according to my perception.

Unlike the slow transition from caterpillar to butterfly, my metamorphosis occurred very rapidly once I got it. I left my marriage and did the unthinkable for a shy, anxious, woman riddled with low self-worth, I took a speaker training to learn to speak in public. Why would I do that? I was being Divinely guided with a strong nudging to do this, not an easy feat for me to accomplish. But I did it and began speaking, creating lectures and workshops about health. Another strong nudge appeared out of nowhere and the message was "Leave your store." "What?" I thought. "I've just gotten the stores (we had opened a second store) going good and customers come in regularly for my assistance. What would they do if I wasn't here? My son doesn't understand how to help the women like I do. Besides, I'm finally feeling good and enjoy the stores even more." But the message continued to say "Leave" and I continued to sweep that message under the rug. No way was I leaving I thought. This is my livelihood and I'm needed. It didn't make sense to me in any way.

However, when I didn't listen, a cosmic two-by-four appeared right out of the blue in the form of my son. Suddenly there began to be a lot of friction between us, something that had never occurred before. He had decided he wanted to make many changes in the mother store and I didn't agree with them. In addition, even though he was in favor of the divorce between his dad and me, it was still a change in his life, and change isn't always easy. In hindsight I feel this contributed to the friction; I was his scapegoat. The friction continued to fester and boil until the pain to remain became too intense. I finally got the message so I said, "Okay, I'll leave, but now what?"

Carolyn's Life Reflection

Here I was, newly divorced and having to do things for myself and the kids still at home that I'd never done before, such as establishing new friends, settling into a new neighborhood and a much smaller house, and now suddenly without a job. In addition my dad had just passed away rather unexpectedly. I felt lost, unloved, frightened, alone, sad, like a fish out of water, but at the same time, I was free. What do I do next was my immediate thought?

An opportunity emerged and a company opened their doors to me. It was to be a volunteer position right then with a promise of a paycheck soon. I had enough income to keep me afloat at that time so thought this a great idea. I was suddenly thrown into a new realm and trained to become a life coach. I learned marketing techniques, and new computer skills, which were sorely needed. Working hard and long hours became my way of life. I felt appreciated and needed and my position rose to an executive role, and finally a partnership. Months went by but no paycheck, but I was still being promised it would come and asked to hang in there a little longer. By now I had put a great deal of borrowed money into the pot, but was again promised that it would be returned.

More months went by and an unsettled feeling began to pervade me. Something was amiss and I realized that the people in leadership of the company were indeed not whom they seemed to be. I was strongly nudged to step away. I also had to find a way create an income since this had never materialized with this company, and living on the earth requires such a thing. It also became apparent that the money I invested would not be returned and I would be left with the responsibility to repay the lenders. My foundation was substantially shaken and felt like it was turned upside down, for I had put so much trust in the people in this company and the principles they had shared.

I stumbled around a while and even hit the ground momentarily, but over the following months I picked myself up, brushed off my knees and took off on my own path rather than someone else's. As I thought back on those last three years, a great realization came to me. I had received a very expensive education in life that was teaching me great truths. Up until then, I had been giving away my power to everyone else because I didn't think very highly of myself. I was needy so had attracted these situations so I could learn how to stand firmly on my own two feet and understand my worth. My own beliefs of guilt, shame, anger, and hurt, had brought me lessons so I could grow into who I really am and could become. Everything was my choice.

From that point on my life became extraordinary and I began to fly. I was writing and self-publishing inspirational/self-help books, teaching classes, coaching, and helping many others move through their challenges with the principles I had learned through my experiences thus far. The old patterns in my life were easy to see in so many others' lives. I knew that because of my experiences of low self-worth, illness and the subsequent journey of healing it, near financial disaster, misguided trust that shook my newly established spiritual foundation, and even the transition through my divorce into a new way of living, I would be able to help these people who were struggling.

Carolyn's Life Reflection

Each experience in our life is a step, and that step can take us into a higher level of awareness or keep us stuck right where we are. Sometimes our choice might even spiral us downward into an abyss. Recognizing each experience as an opportunity to grow into something better removes the negative aspect of it. As I transformed my beliefs of life from a struggle to seeing it as a glorious journey that is an awesome adventure, much shifted within me. I became happy, not because someone appreciated me, not because I had accomplished something and was now worthy, and not because someone loved me, but simply because I finally understood my heritage. As a child of God, I was already a magnificent masterpiece who was born with the power of God within me. I was so loved just for being me, and my responsibility was to spread that love outward. Of course this meant I had to discard all those ugly feelings of guilt, shame, hurt, and unworthiness, for they didn't exist except in my mind. I was created from love so that is my essence.

This was a powerful revelation for me and it can be for you as well. Stop and think about this a minute. You have been created by the Creator of the universe, so are part of that power. It means you are a co-creator of your life, and having this power allows you endless possibilities that have no limits. You are also created from love and do not need to accept the fear of the world. As I accepted this truth doors opened for me that were beyond my imagination, things I would have never dreamed as possible. The mere fact that I had become a public speaker was a phenomenal happening, for I assure you it was never on my original list of possibilities.

In the few years before this metamorphosis of my life, I had been realizing some astonishing things. One was that I had the gift of channeling healing energy and another was an open connection to the angelic realm. Repeatedly I'd hear messages, from where I wasn't sure at first, but the things told to me would come true quickly. Once I realized where these messages were originating from, I was in awe of this gift. I began to journal some of the messages, and days or weeks later, what I had written would happen just as I had written it. This was blowing me away. One day, an angel appeared to me in visible form and I learned she was my first guardian angel Hope—a startling experience. Was she real, or simply a dream? A few months later, during an energy session with a gifted man of healing, he described the angel I had seen exactly as I had seen her, and he knew nothing about her. He described her as she stood in the room with us. Now I was convinced she wasn't a figment of my imagination.

Shortly thereafter, I began working with people in their own healing, recognizing I was able to channel Divine energy through me to them and assist them with releasing blocked energy that was causing their problem. I was able to see things in their past and even some future possibilities, and at times could see someone on the other side who wanted to share a message with the person with whom I was working. All of this was beyond amazing to me. I cannot explain how I can see and do any of this, I just know I am able as long as I'm open to the flow of it and do not try to force or block it with my own mind. Changes were occurring with clients and their lives were improving. This was exhilarating to me as I observed them. What a magnificent gift this was and I continued to be humbled and in awe of it. I remembered a vision I had some years before. I saw myself as owner of a healing center with various practitioners involved in the center. Many aspects of the center were given to me with an understanding that it would unfold when the timing was right. The center would be called Where Miracles Happen.

When I looked back over these last few years, it was hard to believe there had been so much change. I was not the same person by any means — my children will attest to that! The things that had seemed so important earlier in my life no longer held the same meaning. My focus was on helping people improve their life and improving mine in the process. Material acquisitions did not hold the interest of the past, and although I enjoy nice things, it was no longer my quest to attain them. I had redirected my energy into working for me rather than giving it to everyone else, and I had learned that I had to fill myself up before I had anything to share with others. In addition, I was now filled with meaning for my life.

All those years of restlessness and yearning for more had given way to complete internal fulfillment in the knowing I had everything already within me, and there was no need to produce anything to be accepted.

This was another new concept for me because I had been taught it was necessary to give to others first. During my growth I came to realize that if I did not take care of myself first I would have nothing to give anyone else. This had proven true when I became ill since I had given to everyone else and left nothing for myself. Remember, you cannot give what you do not have. Suppose a friend needs $100 and you desire to help this person, but you realize you have less than $20 to your name. Get my point? You cannot give what you do not own! Therefore, I had to develop a real love and appreciation for myself before I could do the same for others.

I became an empowered woman, capable of living my truth and no one else's. Most people live their life through the eyes of someone else, but that is living small. I chose to live grand, and that had to come from being empowered. As a result, I wrote my second book, *The Realness of a Woman*. More and more connections appeared, more opportunities surfaced, and more wonderful like-minded people showed up on my path. My life was rich and full, however I was still struggling financially. That was a puzzle to me at times, but I knew there had to be a block somewhere that I hadn't let go, and the block was keeping prosperity from reaching my door. I had decided to downsize my residence to help the situation.

A huge shift . . .

One day, while in the midst of a 'pity party' for me, I decided to sit quietly and pour my heart out to God and the angels. Tears flowed as I shared my predicament. I mentioned how I was working hard, that I had been following my guidance, that I was discouraged because I was still struggling and I didn't understand why abundance was not flowing to me. As I sat there, absorbed in my own feelings of despair, I suddenly experienced visions of the abundance in my life. I was reminded of all I had—my home, my five wonderful children, my abilities, my clients, my friends, my family, my physical health, my metamorphosis, and even my own magnificence. I was reminded of how far I had come and of all the endless possibilities that lay before me. *Then I got it!* I was already abundant and prosperous. I was actually rich beyond measure and had everything I needed that was of real importance. Immediately a feeling of great peace enveloped me and I was calm and content. I began thanking God for everything. That was it. *I had been focusing on what I thought I didn't have instead of the bounty that was already mine.* At that moment, I heard a voice ask me why I thought I had to downsize my house. I laughed out loud as I answered, "Take a look at my bank account and you'll see why." The response I heard was this. "It is only your perception. You can upsize if you believe it."

I began smiling. Then I thought, "Are you kidding? Okay, if you say so, that's what I really want anyhow," having no idea in the world how that could ever be at that particular moment. My house was on the market and I had been looking at smaller homes, but nothing appealed to me at all. So exercising total faith, I called my realtor that day and told her we'd be looking at upsized houses. Was she ever surprised. The rest is history. Miracle upon miracle showed up, and within a few short months I was living in an upsized home with ease. How did this happen? Here's the key, and it's not just for gaining material acquisitions, but also for gaining anything in your life.

KEY LIFE PRINCIPLE: Whatever you focus on expands. If you focus on what you have and are *truly grateful* for it, it expands into more good. If you focus on what you don't have, you get more experiences of lack.

When I became truly grateful for the abundance already in my life, it was a heart shift that was deep within me, a genuine shift. It began expanding until my desires were manifested. I mentioned this quote from Oprah Winfrey earlier but it bears reiteration; I now know the truth of it. She said, "I live in the space of thankfulness—and I have been rewarded a million times over for it. I started out giving thanks for the small things, and the more thankful I became, the more my bounty increased. That's because what you focus on expands, and when you focus on the goodness in your life, you create more of it. Opportunities, relationships, even money flowed my way when I learned to be grateful no matter what happened in my life." If you understand nothing else from all my words, read this paragraph over and over until you get it. When you get it, you will be amazed at what shows up in your life!

As I put this principle into active use, my life shifted in most glorious ways. As I focused on being thankful, I let go of worry. This allowed me to be peaceful and serene, something that hadn't been my way of life previously. I knew I was so blessed already and had everything I needed. And I was always happy. Sometimes people seemed irritated because I was always smiling, but I thought to myself "How wonderful that I'm known for always wearing a smile." I began to write articles for various websites who had asked for contributions of helpful bits of information to improve people's lives, and I noticed a shift in my focus. Most of the people around me were constantly in a state of stress, and stress is a killer because it tears down physical health—the adrenals, immune

Carolyn's Life Reflection

system, and certainly the cardiovascular system. I had learned that emotional, mental and spiritual components contribute dramatically to physical health, so it only made sense to teach people how to reduce and eventually eliminate stress from their lives. But how in the world could I do that? I figured the best way was to live as an example, but in the next paragraph I'll share with you the simplicity of living life with ease.

When you live in a place of gratitude for everything in your life, and I do mean everything, you accept everything that comes your way as perfect for you. If you suddenly have a financial challenge, there is something you need to learn from the experience. If a physical challenge appears in your life, again there is something you need to learn from it. When your plans are abruptly altered and you are in a puzzled state, there is a reason for it. In this place of accepting everything that comes into your life as good and beneficial, even when it doesn't appear that way, life is serene and stress is not part of the equation.

Let me share an example. I was recently preparing to purchase a commercial property in which I would create the healing center. I was being Divinely guided to do this, something I had known for seven years would manifest into reality. I applied to the first bank and all seemed fine. I waited, and waited, and to my amazement, after several weeks of waiting, I was denied a loan. My first thought reverted back to the old pattern of, "Why is this happening?" All the delay and now expectations shot to pieces in one moment. I experienced a little frustration and some lost sleep while trying to figure things out. I tried investors and other banks but there was always a block of some sort. One morning, sitting in my office chair, I realized I had grabbed back the driver's seat and was trying to make this happen myself. Oops! Old patterns die hard! So I quietly said to God and the Angels that I was letting go of this, knowing it was being Divinely orchestrated and I was in the way. I said, "This is your project. You work out the details because I don't know how to do it, and I'm going shopping!"

While shopping for Christmas gifts that very afternoon, the man I was purchasing the property from called me on my cell phone to tell me he had found another lender. The offer was much better than any others I tried to obtain. Just the fact that the seller was helping me blew me away. I let all of it unfold with no more thought of trying to make anything work, and it worked in perfect timing with no more glitches!

My old pattern was to stress out over the situation when it didn't happen as I planned. Perhaps you can relate to that? For a couple of days, I slipped back into old programming of past years. And guess what—the stewing over a changed schedule didn't help anything. However, when I let go of the entire situation, it unfolded with ease and without stress. Who would have thought that the seller would be interested in helping me find the best offer? It just goes to show that when we get out of the way amazing answers pop out of nowhere.

People in this world are searching. They are searching for love, happiness, prosperity, approval, acceptance, and so on. What I have come to realize along my journey is that these people will search forever and never find any of it until they become what they seek. You cannot love another until you love yourself. You cannot find real lasting happiness anywhere but within you. You cannot become prosperous until you are grateful for where you are now. The only approval and acceptance that will ever be of real significance is what you feel about yourself.

Sure, you can create wealth in your life. You can have a great marriage or relationship and feel love for that person. You can even think you are happy. But these are things of the external world and are not real. The prosperity, love and happiness you really seek can only be found within you. And if it is from the truth within you, it will always involve sharing it with others.

God is my Source, and that is where I find my truth. My life continues to expand and grow. It's exciting to discover where it will take me and I'm willing to move with the flow of my guidance. The biggest challenge is always to let go of any fear that attaches to the new idea and make sure I get out of the way. A seven year dream has manifested into reality as the healing center I envisioned years ago has come to fruition. Some people asked if this was a smart thing to do. Some advised me that it would be a lot for one person to do. Another suggested my age should be a deterrent in beginning this project. Of course, others were concerned if I'd make a go of it financially. Nevertheless, I was directed to move forward with this endeavor so I did. I didn't have this goal for my life, but the idea grabbed me and did not let go. According to Wayne Dyer, this is inspired living, and if you follow the guidance it will always reap monumental rewards that reach beyond the material realm. When inspiration is the light that guides you, there is no stress involved because the doors open effortlessly.

Epilogue

Carolyn self-published her first book, *A Woman's Path to Wholeness*, in 2001, and since then has self-published an additional four books—*The Realness of a Woman, Healing with Color, Angel Love,* and *Seven Roads to Glory*. In addition, she has created and produced three audios entitled *Grab Your Authentic Power, Healthier & Younger,* and *Healing with Color Meditation*. She has created a course that teaches the simplicity of self-publishing and assists many individuals by coaching them through their process. She foresees many more books coming from within her.

In February, 2007, she opened her healing center, Where Miracles Happen. She referred to this seven-year dream in her story, telling how by continually believing it would happen, the dream unfolded when the timing was right. Where Miracles Happen is a place of serenity where people go to experience healing in every dimension, and where they receive much love and support.

Carolyn has created multiple workshops and trainings that include: *Life Skills Speaking Training, Life Skills Coaching Training, Angel Love Practitioner Training, Write, Design & Self-Publish Your Book,* and many others. She teaches classes on health, fitness, life purpose, empowerment, and angels.

Carolyn is happier than she ever imagined was possible and it comes from within her. Why? Because she is living on purpose so is fulfilled to the brim and overflowing, always following the Divine guidance that is directing her path. She is the mother of five, two sons and three daughters, and is the proud grandmother of five—two granddaughters and three grandsons—with three more expected to make their entrance into this world later this year. And Pete, who brings immeasurable joy into her life, and the love they share in their hearts.

You are invited to visit www.drcarolynporter.com for more information. You can contact Carolyn by email at info@drcarolynporter.com.

5

This is Danielle

This is Danielle

Dedicated to God and the ones who need to hear it.
I hope it inspires strength and faith.

How could she go on? Didn't anyone care about her or what she was feeling? She felt so alone; no one would even talk to her. Home didn't feel like home anymore. It was a place of sadness and chaos, not a place she wanted to be anymore. She grabbed the cross and saw and dashed for the woods, crying as she ran. What else could she do? Would anyone even miss her? Gasping for breath she paused a moment, sitting on a broken tree. That's what her life felt like to her, broken, fallen down, unfixable.

She picked up the saw and began to cut. Blood oozed out from her wrist; it was so painful. All those tiny jagged teeth making its own jagged splice on her young skin. It was enough pain to make her hesitate. She was never the kind of person to ever consider suicide, yet in that moment, she realized she was doing that very thing

She had been in pain for so long; she just wanted it to be over. Was this the only way? Was this the best way? Would God want me to do this? Would Mom? Although the prospect of being with her mother was calming, she felt that there were things yet to do in her life. She knew that she was a good person and that she really didn't want to die yet. But how was she going to get through this?

Danielle was born in Milwaukee, Wisconsin, but never actually lived there. Shortly after her birth her parents moved to Texas, but by the time she was three they had moved to Georgia. Mom and Dad got married more as a necessity since Danielle had been conceived and was determined to make her debut into this world. Both mom and dad had been married before, Mom and Dad having three sons and one daughter between them, so when Danielle was born, she was to be the fifth in line. A brother, Carter, was born two years later. Yet even her earliest memories are not of her parents together. After three short years, they divorced and she and her brother lived with mom. A close relative, Raymond, came to live with them shortly thereafter.

Later, Dad found Robbin and married her soon after. They produced two more children, another daughter and son. Danielle had six half brothers and sisters now. Mom found Larry at a bar, and eventually brought him home to live. Larry was an alcoholic. Apparently, Danielle's mom had a humanitarian heart that sometimes made her choices difficult to understand. She wanted to "fix" everyone. So her mission was to bring home many strays—cats, dogs, men, and would pour out her love to them with a plan of fixing them. She always saw good in each person and wanted to bring that good out for all to see.

Danielle's life was far from what one would call normal. Turbulence and chaos were what she knew. Her childhood memories are filled with screaming, fighting, mom's head hitting the fireplace, blood everywhere, flashing lights, cops, mom being taken to the hospital, and her stepmother picking her and her brothers up to take them to her dad's home. Lots of drinking, pushing, yelling—that's what she remembers. To this day, smelling beer sends Danielle into flashbacks as she remembers these unrelenting incidents in her early years. Sometimes she wasn't around and Raymond had to deal with these violent occurrences. He, being older, was protective of Danielle's mom, Brenda, and often fought with Larry attempting to keep him away from her. However, he couldn't protect her as much as he wanted to. He was just too young and small in comparison to Larry.

Her first sexual experience turned out to be somewhere around age four or maybe five. Danielle had a visit from two brothers who lived next door. To her they were quite big, but actually were probably only young teens. She was accustomed to seeing them around the house because they were friends of her brother. One day they came over and found her playing alone in her room. They took her to a bathroom and locked the door. They forced her to fondle them and perform sexual favors. Being only in preschool, she didn't know what they were doing. She was scared and simply did what she was told. They were bigger than she was and she thought this was normal behavior, so accepted it as normal. She never told anyone. She blocked it out of her conscious thoughts until small "snapshots" flashed through her mind many years later. These snapshots indicated that there were multiple occurrences with these two neighborhood boys.

Around this time, another extended family member moved into dad's house. He was in his early teens and a later flash of memories showed her that he had done the same thing

{ 163 }

to her as well. Again, she didn't comprehend what was happening and didn't question it. She simply accepted that it must be something normal people did. Always she was intimidated by the fact that they were so much bigger than she was.

Danielle and her family moved every year or two. Sometimes it was to another state and other times just across town. As she got older, she began to wonder why her mom accepted the abuse of her stepfather. She figured that it was just the way things were supposed to be. Her mom seemed to accept it as okay and unintentionally taught her daughter to think the same.

What made her mother as she was? Danielle loved her mother deeply and they had a close bond, but she realized her mom's life didn't begin the day that she was born. Her mom had her own life story and it included the early death of her own mother when she was a young child, sexual abuse by her stepfather, being locked in closets by an angry stepmother, yelling, fighting, and being made responsible for the running of the household as a young teenager. As Danielle thought about it over the years she realized her mom had simply continued the same pattern she had learned to accept as a child. Danielle thought, "Who am I to deserve better than my mom?" This turned out to be a dangerous conclusion.

Her dad traveled a great deal of the time, but Danielle saw him regularly every other weekend. Since her dad had gained financial success, he had a beautiful house complete with a backyard pool and play-set. The weekends with her dad seemed to provide a short distance between her and the loud confusion of home. Her dad took them out for outings on his boat, drove them around town in a gorgeous restored old-style convertible, and took them on trips all over the country. As she grew older, the occasional trips to Disney and boat outings weren't enough. This wasn't her real life. At the end of all these short visits, she went home to resume trying to be a normal kid amidst the abnormal family chaos.

Yet, as Danielle grew older, she longed to feel valued and appreciated by her father. She needed him to rescue her from the life that she was living, but this did not happen. She and Carter would live with him on occasion when things got especially bad at home, but the kids always returned to their mother. Danielle wanted to be with her mother, but she always felt that her father should have done something to get Larry out of their lives. She didn't know what, maybe have him put in jail for fighting with their mom. Just something.

Danielle hung out with her friends and stayed away from the house as much as possible. However, when she was nine or ten years old, her mom developed breast cancer. She had discovered a lump a long time before but didn't get it checked. When she finally did see a doctor, the cancer was advanced and had metastasized. A mastectomy was necessary. Nothing much was shared with the kids and there were no hospital visits to see their mom. Everything seemed hush hush in an attempt to protect the kids from worry. Her mom went to stay with her sister in Virginia for a while until she recovered, and the kids stayed with their dad and stepmother, Robbin.

After recuperating for a while, her mom returned and they all went home. Larry and mom had separated after the surgery but got back together so her mom could move back home to Georgia and be with her kids. One night, as Danielle was sleeping, Larry entered her room. She remembered feeling her cat being lifted off of her and Larry, reeking of beer, sitting on the bed beside her. Half asleep still, she felt the covers pulled down and Larry began touching her. She looked at him with her half dazed eyes, and he darted out of the room. "Am I dreaming?" she thought. "I must be." This had never happened before. Danielle drifted back to sleep and once again, there was Larry sitting on her bed, removing the covers and slowly moving his hands over her body, attempting to remove her underwear. This time she jolted awake and stared at him with the shocked look of "I know what you're trying to do." He ran out of the room and didn't return. In the morning, Danielle told her mom what had happened. She wondered if her mom would believe her. She did. Larry was given his exiting orders and left immediately. It was a happy day for Danielle with Larry gone; she was so proud of her mom for kicking him out.

Larry was gone and Danielle was just beginning to feel safe in her own home again, when after a short time, her mom met another guy. She introduced Jim to the kids and all liked him at first. He was charming and funny. He really seemed to be a great guy that would be wonderful to mom. It was odd though, his large jagged scar. It decorated a large part of his right cheek. He said that he had gotten hurt in an accident. Later however, it came out that he had been in prison and had received his scar in a totally different manner. Suddenly he was around all the time and within a week or two had moved in. He let it be known that he was there to stay and that he was the new boss. Jim began ordering them around, placing many new rules of can't do this or that. Danielle thought, "Who is this guy to be telling us what to do anyhow? Who is this control freak? How did he get involved in our lives so fast?"

Soon old patterns emerged—yelling, pushing, hitting, abuse—same things all over again. Danielle did not like this guy. In fact, she hated being around him. Larry was trying to make amends with her mom and was calling her. Jim was determined to get Larry out of the picture for good. Mom had confided to Jim about Larry touching Danielle that one night and Jim took full advantage of this knowledge. Bursting into Danielle's room while she was sleeping, Jim told her to get up because they were going to the police station. She couldn't believe that her mom had told this guy her secret. His motives were not honorable and Danielle knew it. Here she was, eleven years old, being drug out of bed in the middle of the night, sitting in her pajamas sharing her story with a police officer who was a stranger to her. It was so embarrassing for her to answer questions the officer asked, "Did he touch outside or inside your panties?" She was horrified. She hated Jim even more after that. Her thoughts were, "How dare he barge into our lives and have anything to do with this?"

Things became worse and worse at home. The fighting was non-stop and the kids saw something different in their mother this time with this guy. Everyone had become accustomed to the arguing of the drunken stepfather and mom. They had grown up with Larry's personality and for the most part learned to live with his alcoholic rants. However, this

Jim guy was different. He scared their mom and they could see it. Of course, as mothers do, she tried to act as if things were okay, but they knew. They knew.

He had no qualms about yelling and shoving Mom in front of the kids. That was part of his plan. Fight in front of the kids. Intimidate them so they will obey. Sometimes he would shove her and look at them with an eerie smile as to say, "If I can do this to your mother, what do you think I could do to you?" The creepiness of this man was difficult to live with.

Mom refused to sign over the deed of the house to him. This took guts because he was a loose cannon. Mom tried to get him to leave but he would not go. He threatened to kill the whole family more than once. Jim had convinced mom to purchase a gun to defend herself if needed against Larry. It had been hidden between the mattress and the box spring. One cool fall day, Danielle and her mom arrived home to a ransacked house. Their first thought was that they had been robbed since everything was turned upside down. Suddenly a horrified look spread across her mom's face and she flew up the stairs two at a time. Just what she feared—the gun was gone. The mattress was flipped over and no gun was to be seen. Both of them were beyond scared. Where was he?

Days went by with no contact from Jim. Danielle's mother worked in an office and was attending a Halloween function there. Who showed up? Jim did, wearing a black ski mask and carrying a gun, a real one. He quietly whispered in her ear that he was going to kill her and her kids, then left. He stole her car and strangely was never seen again. The family lived in constant fear for months wondering when he would make his move. He would call every once in a while to rattle them. Mom changed the phone number to unlisted but somehow he talked the operator into connecting his call to them. That was it. They had to move. So they did. Years later, mom got a collect call from him. Just enough contact to let her know that he was nuts and still around.

Raymond, who now lived with them, had an obsession with pictures of half naked women and had them plastered all over his walls. It wasn't just one or two, there were many all over the room. To Danielle, it was revolting and she hated to look into his room. What puzzled her is how her mom could allow him to do this. After all, there was her young brother who was watching all that went on and being taught that this is fine. She often wonders if this obsession left unchecked and considered acceptable ultimately led to what happened next.

It was a simple command in the silent dark of night, "Turn over." That's all that was said as she barely awakened half dazed from a peaceful slumber, as the rest of the house slept. So much pain, debilitating pain. What was happening? Raymond was there and she had lost her virginity. She was in the midst of puberty and was aware that this wasn't right, but, like so many incest victims, was too stunned by the predator. She also shared that she had felt this strange misplaced feeling of loyalty to him because he was family. She didn't want to upset him by refusing. After all, this is someone she would have to see and deal with frequently. Making him mad would only make it worse for her. So she lay there, still and quiet. It was over. For him. Not for her.

After, alone in her room, she felt so dirty. "Why didn't I say anything?" she thought. Tired and hurt, she began to get angry, first with herself but then finally at him. Even though she didn't utter the word " No," she knew deep down that he should have never forced her do anything like that. The next morning she told her mom of yet another nighttime incident. As a result, Raymond moved away to a different state to live with other family members.

At the young age of twelve, Danielle fell in love. Their relationship was intense and emotionally intimate. They were always together. Although David was only ten, he seduced her with amazing love letters that seemed to be written by someone much older. He even wrote them on scented paper. She has kept them all these years. She had never been given this much flattery and attention. She loved it and him as much as a twelve year old can at that soft age. He was her first love and her first experience in an intimate relationship. She was young, he was even younger. Neither knew how to be in a relationship in a mature manner. In time the fighting began, resembling what her mom had exemplified all of her life. The boy was very jealous and it caused tumultuous episodes of yelling and pushing that often ended with many bruises. Although it didn't feel good, this seemed to be a normal relationship to Danielle.

Unconsciously, she had learned how to provoke fights and fight when provoked. She simply learned two bad lessons from her mother. One was that yelling, shoving, verbal demeaning, and fighting was acceptable behavior. Two, was the less understood reason why some women stay in abu-

This is Danielle

sive relationships. It is that they become almost addicted, if you will, to the constant turmoil that it creates in their lives. The drama and abuse became normal to her. When abuse has crossed that invisible line from undesirable behavior to the norm in her head it can almost become as addictive as a drug.

For Danielle, fighting kept things alive, gave her a rush. She had never been in a calm, quiet home setting so she learned to need the chaos. Make no mistake, this was a learned behavior.

Chaos = familiar, comfortable, a rush

Calm = unusual, uncomfortable, boring

It was not until many years later that she realized that living a calm, abuse-free life could be fulfilling and that she could and would be secure in a loving relationship that shows its strength by exhibiting restraint when provoked, and compassion instead of anger.

In the midst of the turbulence of the intense relationship with her boyfriend, and shortly after Jim left their lives, Danielle's mom was again diagnosed with cancer, this time in her spine. Danielle and Carter didn't know how sick she was, only that their mother and they were moving to Michigan to be near her brothers, which meant Danielle would have to leave her boyfriend behind. Even though things between Danielle and David were not great, saying goodbye to her first love was traumatic.

The fractured family relocated to Michigan. Whether it was the fact that she was in the middle of puberty or wanting the attention of boys, Danielle always found herself needing a companion. She became involved with another boy soon after they arrived. The same scenario developed as before—more abuse. But before long the boyfriend moved to Arizona. Another difficult separation took place, then Randy came along.

She was fifteen by then and her mom was very sick. She met Randy, seventeen, right after he had been released from jail for his involvement with drugs. She felt sorry for him, zeroed in on him and the fact that he needed help. She thought that he must have been getting in trouble because he felt unloved. She felt that she could "fix" him with enough love. She was living out her mom's pattern. However, this proved to be the most abusive relationship of all.

Randy and Danielle saw each other every day. With Brenda so sick, she couldn't control anything going on in the household. Danielle and her brother were basically left to fend for themselves. Her uncles dropped by every couple of days. At some point, Danielle's aunt-in-law, a nurse, came to periodically give mom sponge baths and change the bed sheets, etc. Everything was so confusing at home. This was the age for friends, school, and having fun. She loved her mom but never actually believed that she would die. She thought that since mom had been ill before, had an operation, went on some drugs and went into remission, it would be this way again. There was definitely a mix of hope and denial not only for Danielle, but also for her brother Carter, and even Raymond.

Yet, when the family moved to Michigan, Raymond moved back in with Mom, Carter, and Danielle. Of course, this was uncomfortable but Danielle had no choice. She felt Raymond had the right to be with her mother while she was sick since they had gotten close before. Therefore, she didn't make an issue of it. They never spoke of the incident that caused him to leave in the first place. All three kids slept at this home but typically went their separate ways for the most part. They could all see their mom and friend deteriorating, but in an effort to keep their lives from falling apart, they spent most of their time with their friends. For Danielle, this was her way of forgetting and ignoring what was happening at home.

There were adults around sometimes at the end of her mom's life. People would bring boxes of donated food to the house for the family. A few times, meals were delivered from the church. If you talked to the children today, they would all have very different views of how things worked around the house. Carter felt that he took care of Mom a lot but Danielle only remembers him out with his friends or in the basement playing his guitar. Each one, including Danielle, felt that the burden fell to them to take care of mom.

Danielle's mom was in and out of the hospital. Since she had her learners permit now, Danielle was often called out of her high school class to take her mom to the hospital. She loved her mom but wondered why this was her job. The hospital trips were not making her any better. Danielle felt so helpless and so much wanted someone to care. For two years they'd been dealing with this and she wondered if she could hold it together. She felt so alone, as if she was carrying the weight of the world on her small shoulders. How could she continue this alone? There seemed to be no choice but to plow forward.

It was horrible to watch her mother deteriorate day by day. This wasn't the mother she had known for sixteen years. She was puffy and yellow. Her hair was falling out again and there was that funky sweet smell of a sick person throughout the house. Mom occupied the living room in a hospital bed because she could no longer climb the stairs to the second floor of their townhouse apartment. Suddenly, family members began arriving. Later Danielle understood this was a sign the end was near for her mom. People whom Danielle had never met before arrived daily. Then her dad arrived from Georgia. No longer was her mom responsive; she had slipped into a coma. A heavy shadow of gloom hung over the house. People were saying their goodbyes.

Danielle's dad took her for a brief walk, away from the house. As they were walking, he nonchalantly said, "Danielle, she's going to die. What do you want to do? Do you want to live with your uncle up here or with me in Georgia?" The only thing Danielle could think of right then was "Where was a hug or a compassionate word about what she is feeling?" She was stunned. Didn't her father even care what she had been dealing with and now had to face? He only wanted to know where she wanted to live when all she could think about was that her mother was actually dying. She hadn't believed it before, couldn't face that reality. She felt overwhelmed, in a complete fog and panic. Then on top of having to make a choice of where to live, neither one feeling comfortable, she was told that she would have to leave her beloved cats behind.

This was too much, more than her young heart could hold. Leave her cats? No way! They were the one joy she had, a way to give and receive unconditional love that she sorely needed. As she processed all this in the next moments, she thought about her present circumstances. It was just too much, way too much to handle. She saw her options at that moment, and none of them felt good:

She was losing her mother,
Her boyfriend was abusive,
She was losing her home,
She was moving and losing friends and school,
She didn't have a good relationship with her brother,
and she was losing her beloved cats.

"Can't I keep anything?" she thought. "Must I give up everything that is important in my life? And all at once?" She was distraught, beside herself, couldn't think clearly. She left her father's side to make the difficult decision but wanted only to forget every bit of her life at that moment.

Raymond was not at the house as the end drew near for Danielle's mother. They called for him to come. Danielle sat on her mother's bed holding her hand. Over the last few days her mom would weakly squeeze her hand every once in a while. However, on this day there was no response. Everyone felt this was her last day and anxiously awaited Raymond's arrival. He needed to be present. He was part of the family. When Raymond finally arrived, he talked to Danielle's mother for a few moments. She was so still. But amazingly, she rallied enough energy to lightly squeeze his hand as he was holding hers. Then they knew she was still with them.

Family members continued to talk quietly. Danielle was lying beside her mom, holding her hand as she had been doing for hours. She drifted off to sleep for just seconds. She jolted awake to the sounds of crying in the room. "Oh my God" she thought, "Did I just fall asleep and miss her passing?" Everyone thought she had gone when suddenly a gasping breath rippled her chest. She was still there. There was another gasp and finally a third. Three gasps, one for each of the children present. It was over. All the years of pain and sickness were over. It was 2:22 a.m. on October 22. Danielle thought that the time of her mom's departure was so unique with the successive numbers. In a book written by Doreen Virtue entitled *Angel Numbers*, it says these numbers mean, "Have faith. Everything's going to be all right. Don't worry about anything, as this situation is resolving itself beautifully for everyone involved." And it was so.

Danielle's mother had given instructions that when she passed no one was to call anyone outside of the family for an hour. She did not want to be resuscitated and paramedics would try if that much time had not passed. As they waited for the hour to pass, Carter took out his guitar and did what he needed to do. He played for her. It was a beautiful expression of his love and meant a lot to the family. It eased the pain of the moment and added sentiment to the hour.

The next few days went by in a blur for Danielle. She hardly could recall sleeping or eating at all for days. Her mother lay in the funeral home for two days. Danielle got the

This is Danielle

idea to place a cross in her mother's hands in the casket. She wanted it to be special, handmade by her. She went to Home Depot, bought some wood, nails, and a small hand saw. Tears fell as she cut the wood down to size and assembled the pieces to make a cross to be held by this most loving woman, the one who gave her life, made her meals, showered her with affection, made all the holiday decorations and surprises. This woman was the most important person in her life and she was gone from this earth. She would never be able to hug her mom again, sit by her bed and talk about boys and school or go to her with happy stories or teenage problems. No more Thanksgivings, no more Christmases with her incredible meals and special decorative touches. No more birthdays with Mom behind the camera.

The tears poured out now as she felt abandoned and so hopeless. Danielle could not imagine a time so hopeless, nor could she imagine a time in the future when this intense sorrow would not be with her. She wanted it to stop. She grabbed the cross and saw and ran to the woods. Once hidden by the foliage, she began to cut. Each tiny saw blade made its own painful slice as she slowly made her wrist red with blood. Feeling the excruciating pain and watching a small trickle of blood ooze, she suddenly felt as if God was watching her and asking her to stop. She thought for a few moments, realizing that she could do this anytime. It was almost as though she was intentionally tricking herself out of going through with it. Her heart was broken, her mind was shutting down, somewhere inside her came the strong side saying to the weak side, "Just wait, let's see if it gets better. If it doesn't, we can always do it later." It worked as her breathing slowed and she began to calm.

Her mother was a very spiritual person and Danielle considered herself a Christian. Danielle didn't understand why God had taken her mom and she had felt a void of His presence for quite a while, However, there in those deep, cold woods, she felt that God was connecting with her. She wiped the blood off her wrist and slowly walked back to the apartment, slipping in unnoticed.

The next day was the funeral. The family arrived. Danielle passed her handmade cross around the room so that loved ones could write little messages to her mom on it. Then she laid the cross under her mom's folded arms to take with her, something that touched everyone's heart. Danielle had found two identical rings in her mom's jewelry case, so she kept one for herself and placed one on her mom's finger. In this way, she'd be forever connected to her mom. She still wears the ring today. When the casket closed, she knew her mother was gone, gone forever in this life. Danielle's tears came in torrents as she said her final goodbye. This time it was for real; her mom was really gone.

Life would be different now. The only thing that Danielle could do to create a sense of normalcy would be to stay in school and see her boyfriend, Randy. This had been the most violent relationship she had been in but this meant nothing to Danielle. She had been with him before her mom died and she would stay with him after. She had enough change; she needed consistency. Randy was rough and mean but it was what she knew. She didn't want to deal with meeting and cultivating a relationship with someone new. It never crossed her mind to be without a boyfriend for a while. Since she had been dating, she had bounced from one to the next with barely a skip. She always needed that companionship, that male acceptance.

Danielle made the choice to live with her uncle in Michigan rather than to go to Georgia, but her uncle lived two hours away from her school and Randy had been forbidden to see her. Her dad bought her a used car so that she could trek back and forth to finish school with her friends. That's how she continued to see Randy. However, there was a problem with the car. There was a hole in the bottom of the floorboard and the heater went out, so she would drive for two hours with near frozen feet. After all, this was winter in Michigan! Sometimes she'd have to knock a couple of feet of snow off her car before driving anywhere, which made her feet feel close to frostbite. But determination can be a strong component for making something happen, and Danielle had plenty of it.

A couple of months went by and she wasn't hitting it off with her uncle. Their lifestyle was so different from anything Danielle had known before and it wasn't working for her. In addition, she and Randy were at odds again—the continuous saga of on again, off again. So Danielle decided to leave Michigan and live with her dad in Georgia. Her dad drove up to get her and they rode back to Georgia together. Her stepmother and father were separated which left Carter, only 14 years old at this time, to handle himself much of the time while their dad traveled on frequent business trips. He wasn't

{179}

doing well in school and once settled in, Danielle would drive him to school only to discover he would leave the campus.

Danielle's father had so many friends and many seemed to know him better than she did. That bothered her that he didn't make himself emotionally accessible to her after her mom died. She felt abandoned in a way, feeling that making money was more important than she was. Danielle had tried talking with her dad and he would listen attentively, but there was not much interactive conversation. That left her feeling that she was not understood or truly cared for. There just wasn't that sweet, close, father/daughter bond that her friends had with their dads. So Danielle looked to her boyfriends for comfort, affection and conversation.

Pizza delivery girl was Danielle's new title while she was finishing high school. Randy and she had carried on their relationship by phone until one day he appeared on her doorstep. Even though there was always friction between them, there was an attraction that kept them coming back for more. Like a broken record, yelling, hitting, squeezing, and bruises continued. She was never without marks so struggled with the constant battle to cover her bruises or explain them. They broke up again and Danielle moved back to Dad's house. This was the same scenario for over two years—together then not together, continually moving in and out of the house. But in the midst of all this going and coming, a light began shining in Danielle's life in the name of Doug. He was the bass player in her brother's band. Carter did not want to lose his buddy to his sister so he tried every which way to keep this guy from dating his sister, but Doug didn't listen. So in between Randy break-ups was Doug.

Incident after incident occurred, but Danielle always returned to Randy. Why one might ask? Finally, it seemed the relationship was doomed to end. Randy was beating on Danielle and she had enough, so she called 911. He actually grabbed the phone and talked to the cops as well, telling a different story. When the police arrived, he continued to tell them that she was beating him up. Danielle couldn't believe it, and most of all she couldn't understand why the cop believed Randy. She is 5'2" and he's the size of a football player. Besides, she'd called several times before so they had records of previous abuse. But the officer just replied, "Sorry ma'am. Two people with two different stories, we have to take them both in."

That was it! Never again would she let this guy treat her like dirt. She ended up in jail because of him and she had suffered enough. It was definitely a wake up call. Handcuffed, stripped, made to bunk with a prostitute, sprayed down then sprinkled with white powder, totally humiliated, and given a bologna sandwich that shined with a glimmer of green. Well, she had had it. No more of this for Danielle. She was so embarrassed, especially as she picked up the phone to call her dad in Florida. In fact, this episode was the most embarrassing thing she'd ever had to do.

Dad said he'd make a few phone calls and get her out, but she had to promise to never speak to Randy again. She agreed wholeheartedly this time. Dad's business associate came to bail her out and brought his whole family. It was awful. No one bailed Randy out so he remained for months. But dad had made a deal with Randy, something that Danielle didn't know until years later—he had offered Randy a lot of money to leave and never see his daughter again. It worked! He took the money and never bothered Danielle again.

After her ten hours of jail time Danielle returned to dad's house. Soon Danielle found herself uncomfortable there so she moved in with her ex-stepmother, Robbin, whom she adored and who had always been good to her as a child. Danielle and Doug resumed their relationship soon after she moved and they became serious very quickly. After only a couple of weeks of dating, she moved in with Doug and his roommate.

Danielle, trying to provoke him, began the screaming and fighting that she'd always known, but Doug would never fight back. She continued, even shoving him, but Doug remained calm. This was new to her. She had never experienced a relationship that didn't involve yelling and fighting. It took time but then she got it. This wasn't her at all. This wasn't who she really is. She had unconsciously assumed the role so many had demonstrated in her life. She had been programmed to react as she did. Her eyes were opened—not everyone hits. She tested Doug, thinking he would finally succumb and fight back, but he never did. That just wasn't the way he was wired. Danielle often wondered why he hung around with the way she treated him at first. But he did stay. A large wedding followed and her dad proudly gave her away to Doug. It was such a wonderful new way to live. This was

This is Danielle

peaceful and calm, and love was in the air with their new marriage and life.

Doug and Danielle decided to open their own cleaning service. They became successful quickly and worked together in harmony. They were doing well, had money in the bank and were happy. Even still, she had a stomach problem that she had battled since she was a child. She had frequent nausea that seemed to come out of nowhere. It didn't seem to matter whether she ate or not, nor did it matter what she ate, the nausea was constantly with her.

Then it happened—a day with so much nausea that she couldn't work. She freaked out and the panic attacks began. Doug agreed to stay with her throughout this ordeal so work for either of them was out of the question. She sought the help of doctors who gave her prescription drugs for her symptoms. All her tests had come out normal. The drugs made her so sleepy that she slept most of the day. And once awake, the nausea returned. What was wrong with her? Why couldn't anyone figure it out? Crackers and water were her diet for a couple weeks and her normal 115 weight dropped to below 100. After six weeks of agonizing through the latest panic attack, the doctors sent her to a psychiatrist. Danielle had tried therapists before with little if any positive results. She was dubious about trying it again but was frantic for help.

The therapist that Danielle went to see proved to be an earth angel. Danielle feebly walked into her office carrying a blanket and pillow. In her debilitating state, Danielle needed to lie down because she was so weak. This woman made sense and helped her to see some of the patterns from her past

{ 183 }

that were creating her debilitating symptoms. She explained to Doug that he needed to be patient and understanding so Danielle would feel comfortable to talk about her issues and know that he wouldn't leave her. Danielle was terrified about what was going on with her and needed someone to assure her that she would be supported no matter what. Doug offered his support and she began healing in some ways.

One thing that Danielle was able to do was break the chain of abuse that had been passed down to her. She recalled one time when Randy had been hitting her and she had called the police, the judge ordered him to take an anger management course and her to a battered woman's group. She didn't want to go but was ordered to. However, it ended up being really good for her.

She heard all kinds of stories that were so similar to her story. She learned about the pattern of abuse. Everyone always asks, "How could you stay?" The first time you are hit, he says he'll never do it again and how sorry he is. The second time he says it was another accident and you so hope he'll change as he's promised to do, so you take him back. After all, you love him and want it to be okay. Once the third or fourth hitting occurs your self-esteem has been kicked in half multiple times and you've heard repeatedly how ugly you are, that no one else will want you, or that you're no good. Of course, you believe it and the pattern is set. Danielle visualized breaking this chain of abuse, telling herself she didn't need to live this way. And she did it!

Another thing that helped Danielle was taking pictures of her battered and bruised face. Just seeing it in the mirror was no big deal. It was too in the moment. She would think, "Well, it will get better." However, once she took pictures for the police in case she needed them for court. When she looked at those pictures, it struck her very differently. She realized that she was actually one of those battered women. She says that anyone who is ever beaten and bruised should take pictures of it all so they get a better picture of what they have experienced. Even after her bruises and black eyes were gone, she had the pictures to remind her of the pain and the constant cover ups that took place. Think to yourself, "If this picture was of someone else, would I believe this woman was being abused?"

Life improved for Danielle. She was better but still not all well. However, the couple decided to start a family. This was a huge step for Danielle due to her phobia of throwing up, which of course can be part of a pregnancy with morning sickness. Danielle did fine despite her fears and gave birth first to a son, and then four years later to a daughter. Life was busy yet rich. But the nausea continued and sometimes panic attacks surfaced, so it still showed that all was not well with Danielle.

One day Danielle entered my healing center. She was obviously distraught and asked for help. After a few moments of conversation, suspecting adrenal fatigue as part of her health concerns, I invited her into my office to talk. Since illness had broken my health and life (my story is earlier in this book), I had done much research into this problem of adrenal fatigue. Why is it so overlooked? It has such broad ramifications in the body, affecting every organ and bodily system. So I set about to find the answers for my own healing, and as a result I am able to recognize the problem and offer help to others on their life journey. As I shared this with Danielle, an amazing look appeared on her face and a smile emerged. She knew that someone else understood her symptoms as a real problem and that it could be fixed. There was new hope.

I explained about some tests that I thought she should have and gave her the names of professionals where she could receive these tests. These tests are not usually performed by traditional medical professionals, only holistic professionals. She used some of our services at the center and sought help in other areas as well. We decided on some coaching to release the anger and guilt issues still hidden within her and she was on her way to wholeness. The human body is so resilient and can heal itself if given the right tools for healing.

THOUGHTS FROM DANIELLE

THERE WERE SO MANY REASONS why I felt inspired to tell my story. One reason is to give hope to people who have been through or are presently going through tough times. I know that when you are in the middle of a crisis, it's very hard to imagine that life could be good. I also know that when you find yourself living in an unfavorable way, it's very hard to imagine that your life could change for the better. I know that when you find yourself betrayed by people who claim to love you, it's so hard to imagine that forgiveness can be your salvation and give you peace of mind. In addition, I know that when you are so physically sick that you can't get out of bed for days, weeks, or even months, it's very hard to imagine your body ever being well and full of energy. I know what panic attacks feel like and how absolutely frightening they can be. I remember being so terrified that I begged my husband to stay by my side and not go to work. I was living in crisis. Are you in crisis?

A crisis is a situation you are living in that is affecting your core stability. It could be a health concern for you or a loved one. It could be the loss of a job or home. It could be the death of someone close to you. It could be anything that makes you afraid for what your future may hold.

When my mother passed away, I was in crisis. Everything stable in my life was being taken away. Although I had some choices, they were not ones that I wanted to make. Combined with the pain of losing her, I had to 'suck it up' and move on. I think it is important to experience understanding, compassion, and have time to heal. I believe that people grieve differently and handle a crisis differently. Some people in my life tried to push me into 'normal' life faster than I was ready to go during my healing time. It never helped. Their push always stressed me out, and actually propelled me backward from my healing process. Tough love is for grounding your teenager when they try cigarettes, not for someone who is trying to survive a trauma. So, if you ever find yourself in a place of caring for someone who is going through a crisis, give them the healing time they need and understand that your timeline of healing may be different from someone else. No one is right or wrong. It's simply that everyone has their own time that is right for them.

When my mom died, I couldn't imagine a time when I wouldn't feel lost. I didn't understand that time does pass, days go by, months go by, then years. Now, many years later, I am married to a wonderful, loving, honorable man and have two beautiful children who help me experience a second childhood of hide and seek, pillow fights, bringing home pockets full of little rocks just because they shimmered in the sun, and catching fireflies in glass jars in the backyard.

The things that I have experienced are all things from which I've learned. The encouragement that I want to give others is to know that as you are going through difficult times, remember that it won't always be that way. Our life changes, situations change, you change; you grow. I know how difficult it can be to believe that things will get better. So use it. Use the situation to become a stronger, more positive, loving person. Believe in yourself and believe you are healthy, worthy of love and respect, and a whole and unique individual in your Maker's eyes. Take comfort in that a Divine being loves you and wants you to be happy.

Take a look around you. You will see there are people in your life that love you, nurture you, and are helping you along the way. Then there are some who I believe are put in your life to test you, and allow you to grow. Each of these people are valuable. They can teach you a lesson and become your greatest teacher. Love is the only way to go. It might require you to be the bigger person. Pray for your family and friends, but also for the ones who have offended you. They need your prayers.

The second reason I shared my story is to invite others to talk about their personal weaknesses and learn their strengths. There is an amazing feeling, a release, when you talk about your crisis or even simply your difficult days. Oftentimes, you may realize that you have actually learned a lesson and can therefore use the opportunity for personal growth.

The third reason I shared my story was to invite others to get to know God the way I do. My mom gave me a good foundation in faith starting as a young child. She took us to church, said prayers with us every night, spoke about the Lord's love and mercy often. I remember seeing her read her Bible until the day she went into a coma.

To parents who wonder if your child will be influenced by what they see you do and what you expose them to, I can assure you they are influenced. To this day, I aspire to make my mom proud of the Christian woman that I have become. The great thing is, my mother probably did not even have the foresight to know that by teaching her children about God's love she would influence her grandchildren's lives as well. She taught me. I teach them. I have faith that my children will spread their love of God to their own children someday. Her faith affected two generations and hopefully even more.

Be kind. Be graceful in forgiveness. Be generous with money and resources. Be gentle with words. Be loyal and live with integrity. Whether you want them to or not, the young ones are always watching, always learning, always becoming someone that they were not yesterday. It's an awesome responsibility. We all will leave our mark on this world, so make sure you leave a good one.

The following is my thoughts about people in my life that mean so much to me. They have each taught me valuable lessons, inspired me, challenged me, and helped to make me who I am today.

MY MOTHER—She taught me that love is immortal, forever. It does not die when two people are separated by Heaven and earth. Their legacy lives on. Who you were, and the lessons learned, can live on for generations. She made what seem like so many mistakes and went through so many of her own personal tragedies that began with the early demise of her young mother. She lived through all kinds of abuse and unintentionally gave me the same high threshold for the same treatment. Even so, her loving self was infused into me almost exactly. I have her strong love of animals which I consider a gift because I believe that blessings come from taking care of God's creatures. Every one of my pets are rescues. They find me just as they used to find her.

My mom did the best she could with the lessons she had learned about herself. She made some unwise choices, but also some good choices. She elaborately decorated the house for Thanksgiving and Christmas. She made Halloween costumes for us after working all day. She let me sleep with her when I had nightmares. She helped us with our homework. She said our prayers with us every single night. The author of this book, Carolyn, introduced me to the term "Earth Angel." To me, my mom was a beautiful Earth Angel.

MY DAD—He taught me that love doesn't always show itself in obvious or typical ways. I grew up feeling somewhat abandoned by him because I had expectations of what

I needed and how he should have responded to my needs. Every time that he didn't say the right thing or do what I had in my mind, I felt insecure about his love for me. This began when I was a young teen and continued for twenty years until I began to recall certain things.

Although, I wanted hugs and long talks about missing my mom, he bought me a car and found me a home to live in so that I could commute to school and be near my friends. He knew this was important to me. He bailed me out of jail, even though he had told me many times that he did not like Randy and wished I wouldn't see him. I did anyway and it wouldn't have surprised me if he had let me sit in jail for a while as a lesson. He didn't. He paid Randy to leave town. If I had still wanted to be with Randy, I'm sure that I would have been furious about the pay-off, but since I only learned about this a few years ago, I know that my dad only saw Randy as a persistent problem in my life and wanted to rid me of it.

He always let me return home time after time when I couldn't make it on my own. He helped me monetarily when I really needed it. He even stayed with his head poked halfway in the delivery room at the birth of my second child because I asked him to. That was a big one for him. He is an old-fashioned man where that's concerned. He wasn't even in the room when his kids were born many years ago. When I think back to how uncomfortable he must have been to do that for me, I realize how wrong I was those times thinking that he didn't love me. He did, he does. He expresses his love in ways that he knows to do. Now I realize that if I had seen that so many years ago, I would have spared myself so much pain and the feeling that I wasn't good enough to deserve his love.

MY STEPMOTHER, ROBBIN—She taught me that there are people in this world that show up unexpectedly and give so much of themselves. She was clearly put here on earth to show love and support to others. She was always good to me and my siblings. She married my dad and became a stepmother to six children all at once. Not having children of her own yet, it was amazing how well she got along with us and loved us as her own. She was gentle and compassionate and never made us feel threatened by her relationship with our father. She even took us in many times when things were out of control at Mom's house. We lived with her and Dad while my mom was recovering from her mastectomy and undergoing treatments. She did it with love and made us feel at home.

After a few years of marriage, Robbin gave birth to my sister, Ashley, and two years later, a son. Jonathan was her greatest challenge but also her most fabulous triumph. My brother, Jonathan, was born with some mental and physical disabilities. The doctors, to this day, don't know what happened or why he is the way he is. They did all the blood tests, all the exams, and had no answers as to why. I remember talking with Robbin as an adult, sitting at my kitchen table, with her telling me that she was told by doctors that Jonathan, then a year old, would never function in society, and perhaps walk but not be able to talk well. They actually told her it would be best to put him in an institution and try to move on without him. Can you imagine someone telling you to just forget about your own baby?

This is Danielle

She walked tearfully out of that office and was bound to love her child and prove them wrong, very wrong. She took him to many kinds of therapy—physical, speech, social, and today he is a wonderful, loving, twenty-one year old functional man living in a group home with other moderately disabled men. Jonathan and the other residents go to work five days a week, engage in many social functions and live independently of their parents. The doctors never dreamed he would be able to do this, but a mother's love influenced and ultimately changed his future from white walls to football games and rodeos. She is an earth angel. Even after my dad and Robbin divorced, she kept right on loving us. Robbin and I have remained close and enjoy a wonderful relationship. My kids call her 'Nana', a very southern, coveted name for grandmother. I feel so blessed that she loves us all so unconditionally.

MY BROTHER, CARTER—He taught me that people handle pain and crisis differently. Growing up in the same house, you would think we would have reacted similarly to our less than perfect home life. Actually, some things were similar. We both spent as much time with our friends as possible and we both felt as if we were the sole caretaker of mom. But after she passed, he began to push away his memories of her. What he could recall was the couple of horrible years when she was very ill. Since she became ill when he was so young, he didn't want to remember those painful events, the memories of her began to fade and are almost gone today.

He and I had a difficult time resonating because he wants to forget all the bad memories, but I want to remember my mother so badly that sometimes I find myself pushing those memories on him. He has finally become comfortable with a few mental snapshots that he has left of her. So many of his clear memories are of her sick and there are only a few happy ones. He was so young when mom passed, only 15. It seems to work better for him to release all memories.

However, I hold on to all of the memories, painful and happy, because I'm afraid that once I begin to forget any details, my memory will fade completely. I don't know who has a healthier approach to remembering mom. I have learned that people handle the same experience very differently so to be truly loving to someone, you must respect their way of coping. It's wise to give each person their space and not attempt to force your own way of healing on someone else. Carter and I have become much closer now that I have stopped trying to make him remember things that he would rather not remember or is not ready to remember.

RAYMOND—He taught me that forgiveness is essential and can be life-changing to both the offended and offender. We did not get along when we were children and living in the same house at times made it worse. Then, of course, once the sexual abuse happened, we were even more emotionally estranged. After mom died, we went our separate ways for a few years. It was only when I became engaged that I took a step that some people don't understand. I called Ray as if nothing had ever happened. I told him about my fiancé and invited him to the wedding. Some people asked why I would invite someone who hurt me so badly back into my life. This is difficult to explain. I realize that this reunion may not have turned out as positive as it did. I felt the need to reconcile before my wedding. It meant a great deal to me for all my siblings and close family members to share that day with Doug and I. Ray was surprised and touched that I cared enough to invite him that now our relationship is better than it's ever been. He told me how much it meant to him that I made the first move and reached out to him. He said that he thought that I might not want to see him again.

My mom had taught me about forgiveness. She looked for the goodness in people. Even though she was treated horribly by some people, she still found the strength with God and within herself to forgive. I know that at times I have hurt the people whom I love most. I have acted selfishly as though the world revolved around me. I have even become judgmental towards others and used hurtful words when frustrated. When you grow up with a rough past like I did, it's hard not to have the attitude that the whole world owes you something. I've met others who feel the same way. It is sad to see how it holds them back from succeeding in life, with their relationships, their jobs, even their spirituality. When I am going through hard times, I have to fight the urge to feel sorry for myself and expect that everyone around me will fix the problems for me. It's such a self-destructive way to live.

Let's step back to forgiveness. I never feel that domestic abuse is acceptable and would tell anyone who is in that situation to get out. I have been there and it never got better, only worse. I am thankful I got out before I was seriously injured or killed.

I felt the need to talk to Raymond to see if the estrangement between us could be resolved. My mother was such a loving person and all about family. I also wanted to be loving. So, I gave Raymond the chance to take responsibility for his actions. Not only did he do this, but he did something that I never really expected him to do. He apologized. I had hoped that Raymond would admit what he had done when I faced him, but I expected him to be defensive and give me excuses. I even thought he might try to make it my fault somehow. There was none of that. He was embarrassed and felt terrible about it. He didn't excuse himself. He only apologized.

I'm not implying that everyone who is abused should contact their abusers. I'm simply introducing the idea of forgiveness because I know how important it is for mental, physical, emotional, and spiritual health. Even if your experience of confronting your abuser doesn't turn out as well as mine did, you can feel good about yourself for forgiving them. It's their choice whether or not they accept it. We are each on our own life highway. It's up to each of us to do what is right for ourselves.

MY SISTER, ASHLEY—She is my best friend and has taught me what it means to be a good friend. I remember the day in the woods when I was so distraught and lost. One of the thoughts that came to me was how awful it would be to leave her behind. I felt terrible thinking that she would find out what I did and how that might affect her. I also realized how much I wanted to watch her grow up. This, along with the intense presence of God I felt, gave me enough reason to lay down the saw and return home to start my life over again.

This is Danielle

I have praised God so many times for blessing me with a sister who has such an overflowing, giving heart. She has always listened to me without judgment, and has given me graceful advice while sharing my best and worst moments in life. I was so right to want to see her grow up. She has become an honest, hardworking, intelligent, beautiful woman whose strong faith has been able to inspire me so I can show my love for the Lord as she does. My sister, my friend, my blessing.

MY SON, my first born—Any parent knows the amazing feelings of holding your baby for the first time. It has taught me how wonderful it can feel to put others needs before yours and give of yourself so freely and honestly.

MY DAUGHTER—She is a tiny version of me. It's humbling. Before she came, I was not used to having someone else as strong-willed as I am in the same house. If you ever think that you always have the upper hand, try living with another personality just like yours.

My kids are my legacy. My love for them is true and honest and so easy. It's not that I like everything they do—I don't like the squabbling—but it's so easy to love them. Their beautiful faces and innocent hearts have inspired playfulness in me again. They are the crystal blue sky behind my rainbow.

MY HUSBAND, DOUG—He has taught me about loyalty, integrity, working together as a team, and being a family. I'm convinced that God knew what I needed and gave me Doug. He blessed me with a man, even though I tested him, who never pushed or hit me. A man who didn't leave my side when I was sick, scared, and panicked. A man who knew my past and loved me anyway. A man who called my father to ask for my hand in marriage. A man who works hard and long hours to give our family a wonderful home, food, clothing, health insurance, vet bills, soccer and baseball tuition, birthday and Christmas gifts, while always working in integrity, doing things right. A man who loves the Lord as I do and feels the responsibility to pass that love on to our children. A man who is dedicated to our marriage and will fight for it with honesty, loyalty, apologies, and forgiveness. A man who loves me, just as I am. A man who has already given me ten wonderful years of marriage.

Thank you, Doug.

Love, Me

Epilogue

Danielle continues to improve her health and is feeling good about life in so many ways. She lives with her husband Doug and her two children. Being a wife and mom means everything to Danielle, and her life is full and overflowing.

Helping others is something dear to Danielle's heart. Sharing her story is a first step to reach out to others, which is something her heart desires. She wants to empower people with their personal journey of healing by offering assistance as they ask for help. By God's grace she is healing in profound ways and her desire is to help others understand how they too can heal.

Danielle knows she has endured many difficulties in her life, and her goal is to use the wisdom and knowledge she has insightfully learned for the good of others. She welcomes opportunities for serving others and is open to receive how God wants her to be of service. Her heart reaches out to battered women and survivors of sexual abuse, and she has a passion for the care of animals. She believes that all of God's creatures need love and should be treated with kindness.

If you would like to contact Danielle, you can reach her at DanielleCares@comcast.net.

6

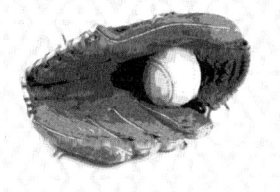

From Beverly's Heart

From Beverly's Heart

Dedicated to Carolyn Porter, whose love and spiritual teaching allowed me to discover my passion and experience true happiness of being Barrett and Bradley's mom. Also, I thank Marc for the gift of our sons and the true love we shared.

※

A BEAUTIFUL LIGHT SHINES SO VERY bright in Beverly's heart—that light is her nine year old twin boys, Barrett and Bradley. Nothing gives her greater joy than to see those two smiling faces with their "Bogus Eyes" (big eyes) grins, a mischievous twin partnership of "Guess what we've been up to Mom?" Motherhood is her life and it is all she had hoped it would be and more. She waited a long time, a very long time, until she was forty-five for these boys to show up in her life.

Every day is an adventure, that's for sure, for as parents who are reading this know, kids can create the unpredictable. And what do moms lack the most? Time. Time for themselves that is. After struggling with this for the past seven years, Beverly has learned to balance her life as much as this is possible. In between throwing baseballs, going on kid-focused outings, helping with the children's homework, and reading her twins their favorite stories, she now allows a little time for herself. That is not an easy task as a do-it-all-by-yourself mother, but Beverly is happier than she's ever been!

Her boys have learned that if they want more of mom's attention they need to help her in the kitchen and with various tasks around the house. "It's working well!" Beverly told me. They often ask her how they can help and their assistance has substantially lifted the weighted feeling of not enough time. Or maybe it's really because she feels they are a team working together for the good of all!

In this way, Beverly has created a happy environment for herself and her boys, who are her greatest gifts on this earth. Her life is rich and full with these two gifts, and she has moved way beyond material acquisitions and career accolades. She has learned what is most important for her life and is now allowing it to unfold for the good of herself and her boys. Her passion is to raise self-confident, respectful and responsible boys who will be able to give a lot to our world.

Raleigh, North Carolina, is where her story began. Beverly was born and raised there until she left for college. Her father was Greek and her mother from England. They met during the war, got married in England, then came to the states and were married again according to the Greek tradition. Finding acceptance by the family was difficult for her mom since Greek parents usually select a wife for their sons. Over time however, she became part of the family.

Beverly's parents took over the grandfather's restaurant and remained in the restaurant business their entire life. In addition to Beverly, there was an older sister Patricia, born 18 months before Beverly. Beverly does not recall much of her early childhood. She seemed to create her own little world and was oblivious to much that went on around her. The girls were taken to the restaurant often and while Patricia was active and into everything, Beverly was quiet. She was given a blanket, a bottle and pop beads in her crib which kept her content until she was five years old. This programmed her to be introverted, quiet, non-communicative with others; she stayed out of the way. Later in her life, Beverly saw this pattern emerge frequently.

One time Patricia decided to "borrow" her mother's make-up and create a new look for Beverly. There was lipstick and powder everywhere—over Beverly's face and body, the crib, the room—you get the picture. Patricia was daddy's girl and Beverly was mommy's girl. Beverly was quite dependent on her mom; she feels her mom liked this and considered it to be a type of security.

Beverly's dad was very loving and giving; everyone liked him. He would give the shirt off his back to anyone in need. Often winos came into the restaurant to get a 65-cent bottle of wine. He would give them food—pinto beans and cornbread—because his motto was "No one goes hungry around me." So it didn't matter whether they could pay or not, they were fed. Sometimes however, dad gave too much away and people took advantage of his generosity. Beverly adopted this trait of her dad's—a giver. She says that she loves to give and I can attest to her generosity with me at times. Now she also learned along her path that sometimes she over gave and people would take advantage of her generosity. Some people grew to expect it. In recent years she has learned to give at a pace that suits the better balance she has created in her life.

Beverly's dad had a drinking problem. He wasn't aggressive or mean, but would often embarrass her with his comments and behavior. Because of this she seldom brought friends to her house for fear of being embarrassed. Beverly never respected him during his drinking years. Not until much later in her life did she come to have the respect you should have for your dad. It was not until he quit his drinking and she saw another side to him she had not seen before. True respect then bonded them.

Since Patricia and Beverly were opposite personalities, one quiet and one not so quiet, they didn't really play together that much. However, Beverly remembers her sister always being there. Sometimes they ran around together just because they were sisters. But always on Sunday's they were together, because the family attended church, all in their proper attire with matching dresses, shoes, gloves and hats. Mom was a stickler on clothing and accessories matching, and they were dolled up to a tee always. After church, they all went out to eat and then to their grandmother's house to visit with their aunts, uncles and cousins.

Dad ruled over the family. He was the aggressive one and made all the decisions. Mom never spoke her thoughts and always held everything inside. She has a dependent, passive personality. Seems like the old patriarchal belief system played out in their family in a big way.

High school opened up a whole new world for Beverly. She tried out to be a dancer in the marching unit and made it. As a result, she got to know the "in" crowd and became one of the group. She had so much fun and opened up to people.

She felt like a butterfly who was just out of the cocoon. She had two close girlfriends, Sandy Pearce and Debbie Brewer, who remained friends long after high school.

And there was first love—such a special feeling. It hit Beverly full force when she met Val. He was Hawaiian, tan and good-looking, and they became inseparable. She loved his family and spent as much time at their house as was possible. But as high school ended, so did the romance.

Off to college, but wait a minute. It was Beverly's dream but the money wasn't there for her to attend. Determined to attend, she set about to earn the money needed to go. After graduating from high school she worked for Buffalo Tire Company for two years until she earned enough money to fulfill her dream of college. She ran the office and kept everything organized for the three male salesmen at this place. The guys were a great deal of fun and she enjoyed every minute of this job. The guys hated to see her leave once she'd earned the money she needed, but they were glad she could fulfill her dream. They wished her well.

She was off to a two year college named Wyngate, located in Monroe, North Carolina. She majored in history and minored in business. During the summer and Christmas vacations she worked to earn money to pay for her college expenses. She found a job working for the state with a man named Don Beason, who was Secretary of Commerce. She gives great tribute to this man. His assistance helped her remove herself from the emotional drain of family issues which he may have experienced and recognized in her. He taught her in most extraordinary ways about the ins and outs of be-

{ 207 }

ing a woman in the business world. He taught her how to be strong and handle herself with confidence. And most of all he allowed her to see she could do it, something she had not known before. He taught her to move forward and never limit what she could do. Every Christmas and summer she worked for Don until she graduated.

After Wyngate, she and her roommate Luan Cox, attended Chapel Hill, but it proved way too large for them and they quickly transferred to Queens College in North Carolina, an all girls school. She graduated from this school with a degree in history and a minor in business.

The business world became Beverly's life. Upon graduation, she was offered two jobs of interest to her, one in Raleigh and one in Charlotte. Her dear friend and former employer, Don Beason, advised her to take the Charlotte job so she could be away from family and strike out on her own. She took his advice, and with the $800 she borrowed from Don (which she paid back within the year), she moved into an apartment and began her new life on her own.

The bluebloods of Charlotte welcomed Beverly at Southeastern Savings and Loan, her new workplace. Five other people were part of this company and a tight bond formed between all of them that continues today. She handled the business development and procured business accounts for the company. It was a good start for her career, but when she discovered she couldn't move up the ladder there, she moved on to a company that allowed her to sell online services to savings and loans.

While traveling to Florida to attend a training, she met a man. At first glance, he reminded her of her first love Val. In fact, until she got up close to him, she thought it was him. She learned he was Syrian—thus the physical similarity to her Hawaiian high school love. He was returning home from Raleigh, and according to synchronicity, she found herself sitting next to him for the trip. She shared a lot of her life, including her dreams, and although the conversation felt good, when he offered to buy her a beer as they exited the plane, she felt it too forward and refused. However, he had asked where she worked, so he began sending her cards to her workplace. He had actually stayed in the Royal Villa Hotel where her parents worked and her mom was cashier when he paid for his meal. Small world!

Russ decided that day he would marry her, unbeknownst to Beverly of course. He was full of charisma and visited her on several occasions. It was one of those back and forth long distance relationships. Russ was a politician, debonair and polished. He wined, dined and diamonded her. He even told her about his similar goals to hers, which she later discovered were created to impress her and held little truth.

The company where Beverly worked announced they were going out of business, so after working there only one month she was now unemployed. This meant a big change for Beverly along with the other changes that were concurrent in her life then. She loved him, but it wasn't a deep, connected love she later realized. Right before their wedding, she went to visit him and he was sick. She saw a different side to him, a selfish and controlling side, but she went into denial and figured it was because he was not feeling well. But it bothered her and it apparently showed on her face when she returned home. Her dad even told her she could call off the wedding if she had second thoughts, but she glossed over it saying he wasn't himself because he was sick. What she later learned was *you should listen to your gut feeling and go with it!*

A big fat Greek wedding took place with lots of food, dancing and lots of relatives and friends present to celebrate. But from that moment on everything changed. Beverly knew on their honeymoon she was in trouble. As they were driving a truck with their things back to Florida, they got lost. Beverly thought it fun, kind of an adventure to find the correct route, but Russ became angry and yelled at her. Arriving in Florida, they boarded their honeymoon cruise. All had changed; he became tight with the money, even to becoming irate when she ordered a drink with the money they had been given as a wedding gift. It was then she discovered he was controlling and manipulative, a totally different picture from what he presented during their dating time. She realized she should have paid attention to her gut feeling when she visited him before the wedding. So listen to your gut feelings!

Beverly believed that once married you make it work. With her Greek Orthodox background, she had grown up with faith and certain beliefs, but Russ felt a woman's place was behind the man—subordinate. She continued to feel this attitude from him frequently. The hard part for her to understand was the complete turnaround that happened as soon as the wedding took place. Other times, it seemed better, so she persevered.

Their life was consumed with political events—meetings, dinners, and conventions, all out in the public view. That is the life with a politician husband, not much time alone. He was the State Committeeman for the Democratic Party. So he was careful when he hit her to do it light enough that there were no bruises, only slight red marks. She would threaten to leave and he'd turn from being the lion to a gentle little lamb, for a while. But this kind of thing continued, one thing after another, and Beverly was getting tired of this abusive life. They tried counseling. The counselor told Beverly that he truly loved her, that he was giving her the most that he could. So she had to decide if this was enough for her or not. It would be her choice.

Beverly wanted a job but her husband would hide the car keys when he was traveling so she couldn't go anywhere. One time she managed to sneak the keys away long enough to get a set made for her. As soon as he left for his next trip, she set out to find a job, which she did. This job got her out and helped her see she could make it on her own. She left him. After some months and his continual pursuit of her, begging her to come back, she went back. It only took a few weeks for the same scenario of abuse to return and she knew she wanted out. When he left for his next long trip, she grabbed a few of her things, left Russ a note, and took off. She took what she could carry and that's it. She was starting at the bottom again.

Working at Citizens Federal Bank, she put a lot of energy into her work which helped her forget the failed relationship, but it also helped her move up the ladder very quickly. Her mind and wit helped her create new methods that received recognition from those in high positions in the company, so the president of the bank came to investigate what she was doing. In the end, they implemented the same programs that she had created, throughout all branches. She was on her way!

Her recognition earned her a higher position, one that she didn't feel confident that she could fill. She was moved to the mortgage area buying loans for the bank. It was difficult for her since she had never worked with mortgages before, and she worked directly with the president and executive vice-president. She found herself buying loans from Wall Street firms in New York. Beverly felt unhappy and lost. She didn't understand the terminology or job. So she called a friend who she reported to as a Branch Manager and shared her feelings. He assured her that she had already earned the company a great deal of money so she could "sit on her butt" for the next six months and then he would hire her back. Just knowing she wouldn't have to remain there for long changed her entire attitude. This goes to show how much your attitude affects your life.

Beverly became a different person and over the course of the next six months she went to meetings and conventions, did networking, asked a lot of questions. She learned that her greatest assets were her ability to network, her good communication skills, and that she was an excellent listener; she knew how to handle people. She learned about deals, how to put them together and make them work. She took them to the president and executive committee and presented the

From Beverly's Heart

deals in meetings, and then would negotiate million dollar deals with Wall Street. Not bad for a little girl from Raleigh, North Carolina!

Traveling became a way of life; she would travel to six conventions every year. Tennis she loved and played every chance she could. She bought a townhouse, got two Yorkshire Terriers, and life was good. She had come a long way from the day she left her husband with only a handful of her personal things, and it felt good to be independent. She loved to read; she felt in charge of her life at age 35.

Bob Miller was her tennis coach. He was retired, had moved from New York to Florida, having been a successful car salesman in the company where he worked. At 70, he taught tennis because he loved it, and it was obvious it wasn't for money because he only charged $10 per lesson. He was such a great teacher that she continued her lessons for three years, becoming quite proficient at the game.

Beverly dated here and there, but was mainly out to have fun. She was about to head to Atlanta and meet a man for the weekend to play golf, so she visited a nearby store to purchase golf shoes, gloves and other accessories. There she met a guy named Marc, the manager of the store. He was so nice and even suggested that she didn't need all she thought she needed to buy. That impressed her, and it was obvious he knew his merchandise.

Her weekend was fun; she played golf and hung out with the man in Atlanta. But she continually thought of that nice guy Marc back in Florida. Upon her return, she mentioned Marc to Bob, her tennis instructor. He knew Marc well and

{ 213 }

reiterated what a great guy he was. Bob told Beverly to go back to the store, and playing matchmaker, he immediately let Marc know that one of his students would be coming in to buy something. So Beverly got all dolled up so she looked her best, and went into the store to see about purchasing a tennis skirt. She found a bright pink one and bought it while having conversation with Marc.

After a few days, Marc called to ask her out to dinner. They had a great time and found it comfortable being together; she thought he had a good soul. A few days after their first date, she received a package. Inside was the matching shirt to the tennis skirt she had purchased, and with the shirt was a single red rose with a note that said, "I had a great time the other night. Want to go out this weekend?" They did. They continued to have lots of fun together, laughed a lot, and enjoyed playing tennis together. Some nights she did her own thing and he did his. She had never had this before—no controlling.

When Marc's roommate decided he was moving, Marc had to do the same. He told Beverly of his intended move and she suggested he move in with her. She had made up her mind that never again would she marry anyone before living with them for a while; she didn't want to experience anything that resembled the dramatic personality change or the abuse with her first husband after they married. She told Marc that she'd give this a year. If it didn't work out then they'd go their separate ways because she wanted children and her body clock was ticking away. She was 39 and he was 30. She wanted the old-fashioned dream of marriage, husband, children, mom at home—all of it.

Over the next year it was decided that marriage would be a good thing for them. This wedding was totally different from her big fat Greek wedding with 300 people attending. Bob gave her away; the bride wore her aunt's wedding dress. The ceremony was at 11 a.m. with a brunch following as a small band played during the festivities. A small group of people attended and by 3 p.m. everyone was on the beach for fun in the sun.

Marc left the tennis and golf shop and went to work in the car business as a service advisor. Not long after, Citizens Federal Bank where Beverly worked was bought out. She received four great job offers and one was in Atlanta. Marc was okay with moving so she took the job in Atlanta since that choice had the most appeal for both of them. Marc quickly found a job with Mercedes-Benz, and later went to work with a BMW dealership. They bought a house and one day Marc came home with a motorcycle. He had them when he was younger and loved riding them. He and Beverly went up into the Georgia mountains on weekends and experienced great times enjoying nature. Soon he bought another, a sports bike that went really fast, and he began riding with a group of guys on weekends.

Marc knew how much Beverly wanted children. During her first marriage it turned out that her husband had low fertility, but now she learned that one of her ovaries was not working. They began their journey through infertility issues. She gave Marc three months to think about whether he seriously wanted to pursue this. She didn't want him to feel forced into having children if he didn't want them. He was okay either way, children or no children, but she knew she'd never feel complete without having a child.

This is when I met Beverly. I co-owned a health store with my oldest son. Marc had been coming in and talking with my son about building his muscles, but one day Beverly came in and asked for my help. She told me of her problem with conception and wondered if there was anything natural she could do. Some of my customers had responded quickly and had been able to conceive, using a combination of herbs I had put together after reading many sources. She tried it but after six months it hadn't worked. She went on to try many other avenues and finally, after four years of trying to conceive, she and Marc decided to try in vitro. It wasn't cheap—every attempt has a price tag of $15,000.00 (or more). They would have to use their bonuses to pay for this procedure.

First attempt failed, but the second attempt was a success. Beverly would fulfill her lifelong dream of becoming a mother at the age of forty-five. Soon they discovered there would be twins! Beverly was permitted to work from home. It was a happy time for she and Marc and her pregnancy was a model pregnancy; the babies were due the end of January.

The first part of December something very unusual happened. Marc didn't come home one night. She called his best friend and verbalized her worst nightmare—an affair. His reply was, "Beverly, Marc's affair is not with a woman, it's with a drug. He's taking cocaine." She was shocked; she had no inkling of this. He of course denied it was anything—said it was an infrequent occurrence and that would be it. But a couple more times before Christmas he again stayed out late or didn't come home until morning. She couldn't help but wonder why cocaine. Marc was an avid tennis player, worked out faithfully, ate healthy, took his supplements and was in great shape. Why?

December 27—something felt strange to Beverly; something wasn't right. She told Marc as he was leaving to wash the car not to be gone long because she was feeling funny. Moments later she felt something wet so called her girlfriend asking what was going on since the babies weren't due for another month. Her friend advised her that probably her water had broken and she should call the doctor. By the time Marc arrived home there was no question as to what was about to take place. They arrived at the hospital at 3:30 p.m. and the babies were delivered at 4:30 p.m. All the hospital staff was scurrying to prepare not only for a C-section, but also for a twin delivery. It was an emotional time for Marc at delivery. Beverly's emotions broke loose once she was back in her room. The nurse brought both babies for her to breast-feed. She started crying and wondered if she could handle this with two babies. It was overwhelming at that moment.

Marc took a week off and they had a wonderful week getting to know their brand new sons. He was again the loving, nurturing man she had fallen in love with. However, old patterns die hard and soon Marc was staying out here and there, coming in at 5 a.m. After a while Beverly decided to lock the door. On one occasion, he knocked down the door as she and one of the babies, Bradley, were nearby, and both had to go to the hospital. Bradley was less than six months. Marc was not himself. He had become someone else.

Beverly filed for separation but in Georgia there must be physical abuse for legal separation. She contacted an undercover female detective and staged a set up to catch Marc at his worst. It worked. The boys were at a friends' house, the door locked. Beverly was hiding in the boys shower, and the plain clothes detective on the property waiting. Marc arrived home to the locked door and once again knocked down the door, proceeding to run through the house screaming for Beverly. Hearing the noise the undercover detective raced through the front door and Marc immediately took her on. She put a gun to his head and ordered him to stop or she'd shoot him. Surprised, Marc came to his senses, submitted to her and backups were called. Marc was escorted to jail. After his jail time he was released into Charter rehab facility for a month to detoxify his body and hopefully end his drug habit. Their boys were one year old at this time.

Troubling issues continued for Beverly and Marc. He replaced his drug addiction with shopping, buying $6,000 worth of Versace clothing, a $2,500 Versace necklace and a new motorcycle that was on order. Later Beverly went to a savings account that had $64,000.00 in it and found only $4,000.00 remaining. They were living together, present in body, but not connecting. They were congenial and there for the twins, but after some time decided it would be best to separate. On June 7, 2000, Beverly called Marc right before he left work to inquire about dinner. He replied he had steaks for the grill and was leaving soon to come home and cook them. There was a momentary hesitation, and then he said "I love you more than anything in the world." Her response was "I do too." It was as if both of them felt some feeling come over them simultaneously that they weren't going to see each other again.

Earlier in the day, there had been words between Marc and his boss, Pam. Marc had done something that he shouldn't have and words were fired back and forth. Pam was the kind of person who didn't want a day to end on a bad note, so she asked if they could "make up" before he left. She was well aware of his cocaine addiction and his struggle to be free of it. She told him he wasn't himself that day and his actions were not the Marc she knew. He apologized. She hugged him and he turned to her and said, "I'm not getting a divorce. I'm going home and my wife and I are going to make it."

Time passed. No Marc. Beverly fixed some dinner for herself and the boys. Marc should have been home at least an hour before. Beverly thought he had chosen the drugs again. She said out loud, "I'm just so sad that he can't give up those drugs." She continued her thoughts silently, wondering why if he couldn't do it for her, at least why couldn't he do it for the boys. "We have these precious twins who look just like him. But I can't change him. I have to move on with my life and simply detach so I can make a life for me and the boys." These thoughts rambled around in her head as she sat there at the table. She ate with the boys, crying the entire time.

A knock came on the door. The clock said 9 p.m. She opened the door and a detective stood in front of her. Without thought she said, "My husband is dead isn't he?" He replied, "Yes, but how did you know?" She explained to the detective that she felt it, that she had gotten a strange feeling earlier, and it turned out it was at the time Marc died. She didn't know it was an accident; she thought it might be related to a drug overdose.

Marc was coming home that day, June 7, 2000. It was a beautiful day and he enjoyed riding his motorcycle when it was so beautiful outside. Suddenly, a Corvette turned the corner out of nowhere and his life was over. Marc was hurled from his motorcycle, his neck was cut and he died instantly. Just like that, without a moment of warning, his life ended. Marc wore the best helmet you could buy and leathers for protection, but it wasn't enough. The forty year old driver worked in construction, had no insurance, and turned around and sued Beverly. Apparently there is a no fault situation in Georgia that states that if someone doesn't have insurance the other person must pay.

The detective arranged for a neighbor to stay with Beverly; she couldn't be alone at a time like this. She remembers feeling no emotion. She kept telling herself she had to be strong and continue on, so she simply went through the motions and began calling family. She knew she wanted to write something to say at the funeral in order to share about the wonderful times they enjoyed the majority of the years they were together. She wanted people to remember Marc for who he really was without the effect of drugs—his true self. She had never been mad at Marc for his drug use, but was frustrated and overwhelmed with the additional burden it caused for her. She wanted to leave everyone with the memory of how great a person he was and that we may never know why he struggled with drugs. She knew it was important to share that he was the love of her life and always would be.

There was a great outpouring from family and friends in presence, but once the funeral was over everyone left. Where did everyone go? Where was everyone now that she needed help with the twins and all there is to do after someone's death? Didn't they know she felt as if the rug had been pulled from under her and she was stumbling through a blur from the events of the last few days? After all those years when Beverly made the effort to go home for holidays, weddings, funerals, and special events, why did no one stick around to help her? Marc's death was such a huge shock; she was left to care for two little babies alone—was it too much for someone to stay and help?

But Beverly continued doing as she'd always done, keeping the same routine. She did this for the next six months, traveling to her mom's several times and again at Christmas. Driving home from celebrating the holidays at her mom and sister's house, she was exhausted to the point of falling asleep at the wheel. She had to stop, pay for a motel for two hours to sleep, so that she could continue the drive back home, and then it hit her. It felt like a jolt out of left field. Something is wrong with this picture. She thought how her sister had older kids, her mom is older, but she was the one doing all the running, after working all week, taking care of the babies with no husband or relief. Right then and there she made a decision. All of this was over; she couldn't do it anymore. Her health was suffering and it was just too much. In fact, due to continued female issues, she was scheduled in two weeks to have a hysterectomy.

Beverly would have loved to have her family there to help, but since no one offered she had to hire someone to stay with her to take her of the boys while she recovered, and this to the tune of $2,500.00. What she recognized after Marc's death was that family and friends would call and check in, but rarely did anyone offer to help. One neighbor however, did help, and people brought food. This amazed Beverly, especially since she had always been one to help others, and now that she needed them, not many came around.

The drama was just beginning. The legal matters were another added burden that Beverly had to carry. It took months to sort everything out. She was beyond overwhelmed, not knowing which way to turn or how to get everything done. She felt like a robot, often getting only two or three hours of sleep a night, yet she received her best work performance ever. That amazed her, but she knew she couldn't go on this way; exhaustion loomed over her like a heavy, dark cloud. The financial pressure was enormous. All Beverly's adult life she had created enough money to support herself and live comfortably, while she maintained some money as back-up. Now suddenly she had to support herself and her babies. To her normal bills she now had to add $1,200 per month for childcare and $500 for formula and diapers. She took this task on and did it because she had to, alone. It seemed that no one wished to help her and she felt it was entirely up to her. She quit asking for help and simply grabbed the load and carried it. But there was a cost.

Female problems had remained with her for some years now. After her hysterectomy and sinus surgery in January of 2001, she developed a hernia from carrying the boys around all the time, which resulted in another surgery in March. A few months later, another bulge appeared, another hernia, and a third surgery occurred. Between January 2001 and December 2004, she had a total of five surgeries.

Before the fifth surgery in December, 2004, she endured a great deal of pain with never-ending exhaustion. In fact, it was so severe she knew something would have to be done immediately. She sought another doctor who shared some less than great news with her. Due to her multiple surgeries, the scar tissue that had developed could be causing her terrible pain, or it could be the mesh that was used previously that was causing the pain. When she entered that doctor's office on that day, she told him "If you can't do something to help me I'm going to kill myself." She had reached her limit of pain and could not go on like this anymore.

Beverly's sister, Patricia, and her mom came to Atlanta the day before the surgery. The day after she was released from the hospital, they took the boys and went back to Raleigh, N.C. Beverly was left all alone in the house with tubes hanging down each side of her. I learned that she was alone so took her some dinner. We spent time together, having a great girl visit, since now Beverly was calm and had plenty of time, which had been a rarity in the past years.

The doctor did repair the mess from her previous two surgeries, removed much of the scar tissue as well as a piece of mesh that had been inserted into her abdomen. After months and months of constant pain and fatigue, she began to heal. During all this down time, Beverly had time to think about her life, her priorities, where to go next, something she didn't have time to do in her daily rushed routine. During this quiet time she was forced into taking, she received great new insights into her life. She began reading books again and picked up the Bible and began reading. It was then she realized God didn't want her life to be like this, but instead she was to be full of joy, peace and love. She had not been feeling this because she hadn't allowed time for it. She was not allowing any time for herself because she was too busy doing for everyone else, which had a lot to do with why she had all her surgeries and repairs. With this realization, she knew she had to break the pattern so that she wouldn't pass it down to her boys. She says, "I had to change to be a different person, making me a different mother."

She had sold the house where she and Marc had lived a couple years before and downsized to a nice house, but a bit smaller. She knew she needed to downsize again and take some financial pressure off herself. The company she had been working for, MGIC, suddenly downsized her, and the six months severance pay she received helped her facilitate the move and gave her living expenses for a few months. It was at this time that Beverly became an integral part of my life. She scheduled life coaching with me and we did some angel/energy sessions. It was time for a major change in her life, a shift of priorities and obligations. She knew she wanted to spend more time with her boys. After all, she was all they had, and she wanted to be there for them. Her deepest desire, since she was 28 years old, was to be a mother. Working in the corporate business world did not allow her much mother time.

Seminars, classes, books, coaching—it took Beverly into a higher level of what she wanted for her life and her boys. Her deepest desire was to work with children. And it's amazing how synchronicity plays out if you surrender your desires to God. She was sitting in a doctor's office waiting for her turn. Flipping through a magazine, an ad on a page jumped out and almost hit her in the face. An organization called FastTracKids offered a program for teaching kids literature, science, self-esteem, and public speaking. She called as soon as she left the doctor's office and made an appointment to take her boys there for a visit. They loved it and yes, there was an opening for a marketing person. Again, synchronicity!

Beverly worked there for a year and loved the job, but it was a long day leaving the house with the boys at 7:30 a.m. and returning home at 7 p.m. One night she arrived home with the boys and was so exhausted, so she told her boys she needed to sit a minute. She fell asleep and at 8:30 the boys woke her up asking if she was going to fix dinner. She was totally drained. This time she called her mom for help.

Her eyes became fully opened that night. When her mom answered she uttered "Mom, I'm really sick. I need you to come here and make sure my boys are safe. You don't have to cook or clean, just be here and make sure they're okay." Her mom changed the subject and talked about something else. Again Beverly said, "Mom, I'm sitting here telling you I need some help. I'm ready to kill myself. Do you understand what I'm saying? If I didn't have these two boys standing in there I'd put a gun to my head and kill myself. Do you not understand?"

As if she didn't hear her, Beverly's mom said, "I have to go now but I'll call you later." Beverly sat there stunned, in total disbelief as the tears flowed. "I don't get it" she thought. "What do I have to say to make her understand I'm sick and need help?" Her mom called Patricia, Beverly's sister, who then called Beverly back. Here's what she said. "Mom says you're not feeling well and need help with the kids. If you meet me in Charlotte I'll pick them up." Beverly hung up on her. "Doesn't anyone get it" she thought. "If I could drive to Charlotte I wouldn't be asking for help."

This was a turning point in Beverly's life. She knew without a shadow of doubt that she couldn't depend on her mom to be there. She realized that all those years she had thought her mom was there for her, but she wasn't. She was there in bodily form while Beverly grew up, but not there emotionally. She thought family was supposed to be there for you through thick and thin.

She thought back to Marc's upbringing. His mom left when he was young due to marital conflict and he grew up with his dad. Mom came to visit for holidays and birthdays and gifts came throughout his life, but he never felt his mom's love. Perhaps that is why Marc sought drugs—to fill that empty space within him. His mom loved him as much as she could, but couldn't connect with him emotionally. Beverly surmises that is the reason she and Marc were so attracted to each other. Both had experienced a similar emptiness and gave each other what they had not had as children.

Beverly never realized this until Marc died and she found herself in need. Then she had an acute awareness and realized family had never been there for her. This taught her that she is strong and can manage without family and friends who are not willing to give emotionally or physically. She will make it no matter what by leaning on God as her Source. He will give her the strength to go forward and provide for her family's needs.

Beverly remembers one particular morning when she got up so tired that she was dragging herself to do even the menial tasks. She cried out to God saying "I can't do one more thing. I just can't do it anymore. I'm so tired I just can't do it." God came into the room in a bright white light. God said to her, "I will get you through this. You will make it and I will get you through." She said she felt God's love and warmth wrap around her body like a caressing blanket and knew God was connecting with her. From that moment on her entire life changed. And she knew she would make it. God is now her husband, the father of her children, and whom she goes to for direction on every decision she makes for herself and her boys.

For the first few days after Marc died, Beverly slept with her boys, in the middle between them. She felt she had to protect them, that someone might try to take them. One night, as she was sleeping, she felt someone in the room. She bolted upright. There was no one that she could see, but she could feel a weighted presence sitting on the bed. She realized it was Marc. Had he come back? In quiet words he said "I just want you to know I'm sorry about everything. I didn't mean to hurt you. I'll be able to help you more where I am now. You're a great mother. The boys will be with you and you're going to have a good life. I love you more than anything in the world. I wish I could be there with you and the boys but I can't." Then he vanished. Beverly had been dreaming that she would get to be with him for one more weekend as a special favor from God when he came to her that night. When Beverly feels sad about Marc not being there with them, she remembers this as a mere reflection of the love they once shared and she reminds herself it has not gone away.

A few months later, Barrett, the oldest and most emotional twin, got up one morning and told Beverly "My daddy was holding me during the night. He came to see me. Daddy told me that he loves me so much and for me to tell you he loves you so much." He said it in the same tonal fluctuation as Marc always did—the same way. Then Barrett walked over to Beverly and rubbed her arm just as Marc had so often done, in the exact same way. Chills surged through her body with an electrifying rush. "Oh my God" she thought, "this is how he's getting messages to us." It was a *wow* moment!

Bradley is the quieter twin, keeping things inside more, but also more peaceful. He would calmly say that his daddy is so happy in heaven and how glad he is that his daddy is happy. He continued by saying that he is happy because God is looking after them. Beverly says Bradley is really at peace with everything—you can just feel it. Bradley wants to write a book some day. Barrett has now overcome his anger for not having a daddy like other boys in his class have.

Beverly's life changed so dramatically during this time after Marc's death. She was outgoing and sociable, but learned she couldn't keep up with everything now and had to let go of her social life. She has been amazed however at the dynamics of her friendships. Her friends still had expectations of her and shunned her when she couldn't meet those demands. Beverly had gone from an income of $300,000.00 per year to a mere $30,000.00 per year. It is obvious she couldn't do as before; she soon learned she couldn't be the provider and mother for her children while pleasing family and friends or anyone for that matter. She made a big choice. Beverly chose to listen to God. She asked for her purpose and His direction. God answered that it is to please Him and take care of her children. That is what she is doing. Even when she worked with FastTracKids, she realized she had been giving so much of herself to the children there that she had little left for her own children when she got home. That's when she got it—she needed to work with her own kids first and foremost—everything else was secondary. Before, she would have chosen her job to give her children a better financial life. Now she chooses to give herself to her children, and that's what they want most.

As a result of her life lessons, and the journey that took her through and over many hurdles, Beverly is helping single women who need support through a non-profit organization called The Angel Connection. She and Myra Holland, a woman who had a vision to help these women, are there to support women who want to give more to their children and be with them but have been dealt some heavy blows in life. They assist women with emotional needs, finances, organization, and many other ways. Their motto is "To connect single mothers with God's resources to transform their life." It is not a handout. Women who receive their help must sign a ninety-day agreement that when they are able to be on their own they must pay it forward and help someone else. It's a matter of taking pain, hurt, devastation and needs, and transforming it into all that is good.

Epilogue

To the world, it may seem Beverly went from the top to the bottom, but she knows it was all part of her journey. Sometimes it felt as if she'd hit bottom, but hindsight has shown this was only perception. She experienced material downsizing so that spiritual riches could emerge.

Beverly gives tribute to friends, family, and her church family who did take the time to reach out and give their love and support to make a difference in the boys and her life.

She is happy with her nine year old twins. They have a new home in a place they love. She is a loan originator and does this out of her home so she can be there for the boys when they get off the bus from school, help them with their homework, and spend time together. The owner of the mortgage company for whom she works was also a single mom, and they are able to cut loan costs on fees to provide loans for single moms and others at substantially lower costs. Beverly feels this is only the beginning of what she plans to do to help single moms in the future, knowing all the time that God is providing for them as He has always done. Life is good!

You can contact Beverly at: beverlybogus@bellsouth.net.

7

And Now Kate's Story

And Now Kate's Story

Dedicated to the beautiful, loving, opulent universe,
my children, my family, and the love of my life.

IT WAS JULY 21, 2007, when Kate DuRie stepped into my life. Petite, vibrant, with a sweet smile that radiated from her face, no one would have guessed the story that had tormented and tortured her mangled life for decades. Torn and broken from a life riddled with drugs, alcohol, abuse, deceit, murder, and pain in her earlier life, Kate made a choice. She stepped out of her old story and created a new and glorious life. It was a battle in which she felt beaten and scourged, until one day she said, "Enough is enough. I want more than this for my life. I need help." She found help and forged ahead with the support of God and many loving individuals, until she made it through to a brighter day.

Kate made her entrance into this world in 1961, and was handed to her parents when she was seven days old. Her parents privately adopted her before she was born after learning their three year old son was the only child to whom they could give birth. Living in Columbia, South Carolina at the time of her birth, they chose Kate to join their family.

No one would talk about where she came from. Once she learned of her adoption, Kate naturally wanted to know more. "Where did I come from?" she would ask. But it seemed to be a big secret that no one would discuss with her. So Kate thought there must be something really bad in her background if no one would talk to her about it. She was told her birth mother loved her very much but had to give her away, so when her adoptive parents said they loved her, she lived in the constant fear that at some point they would have to give her away too. Looking back on all of this, Kate believes her parents were advised to say this to her. Adoptions have come a long way over the years, but at the time of her adoption all details were kept as a big secret. Whereabouts or information about birth parents were never to be disclosed.

Kate grew up thinking something was wrong with her, that she must be really ugly, or perhaps she was not good enough. She never felt good about herself.

Kate's memory is of her mom and dad drinking every day. In fact, Kate never remembers ever seeing them sober after 5 p.m. on any day. They would slur their words, meals could become somewhat messy in their inebriated state, and eventually they would stumble to bed. It was not a pretty sight. They also argued continuously even though they loved each other very much. Kate realized over the years that this fighting was simply part of their relationship. In addition, Kate received at least one spanking every day. This was not a happy environment for Kate.

However, there was someone in Kate's life who showered her with love. Ertha was her name; she was Kate's nanny. She came to help them when Kate was about four years old and remained with them until she was nine and they moved to Atlanta. Kate dearly loved her nanny. Ertha would clean, cook, get Kate and her brother ready for school, and basically run their household. She set many boundaries, and it didn't take long for Kate and her brother to understand there would be consequences if they didn't follow the rules. But Ertha was fun, warm and loving, and Kate adored her. It was a sad day for Kate when she had to say goodbye to Ertha. When they moved to Atlanta, Ertha remained behind so she could be near her family.

When Kate was around five years old, she was sitting on her dad's lap and enjoying some quality attention since he traveled during the week and was gone so much. Her mother became very upset and accused her of inappropriate sexual behavior with her dad. She had no idea what sexual was or what her mom meant, but thought she must have done something wrong. This added more fuel to her feelings that there was something wrong with her. Her mom took her to a psychiatrist but told Kate he was a tutor. Kate did not understand and felt shamed even though she didn't know what was going on. These early feelings of not good enough set the stage for the pattern of Kate's life choices over several decades.

A highlight in Kate's young life was her trips to North Carolina to visit relatives. The property where her Grandma, cousins and other relatives lived, was family owned. There was a three-acre Japanese garden, gazebos, swimming, skiing, lots of dinners, a Shangri-La that was a great blessing in her life. They went to this place every summer and Kate loved the time she spent there. One wonderful surprise came from her dad. He took her to a nearby horse farm and told her to pick out a pony. He bought that pony for Kate, and it remained at a nearby stable. Horses are one of Kate's great loves.

Since Kate's dad traveled Monday through Friday, she was home with her mom. When dad came home however, he spent quality time every weekend with his children. The routine was: Dad took her brother fishing on Saturday (or something her brother liked to do), and Sunday was Kate's day. They always went to the stables to ride horses, because riding horses was a highlight in Kate's life. Her dad knew how much she loved horses and how much she missed her pony in North Carolina, so he and Kate's mom bought her a horse, right before they moved to Atlanta.

The move to Atlanta was a rude awakening. Kate and her brother went from home-cooked meals to burned TV dinners. She was no longer receiving the warmth and love from her beloved nanny Ertha. There was such a void in loving parenting. Kate became very independent, walked to school, and even began cooking her own meals. She remembers that the house was not very clean and the produce wasn't fresh.

One time, while visiting the relatives in North Carolina, Kate saw a cow give birth to her calf. She befriended the calf and played with it. The calf, named Sam, became her pet and followed her everywhere, even allowing Kate to sit on its back and hitch a ride. One night, during a steak dinner, her brother cruelly said, "How does Sam taste?" Kate was horrified to realize she was eating her beloved pet, and from that day forward she never ate meat again; she became a vegetarian at nine years old.

And Now Kate's Story

Each of Kate's parents had a different view of money. Her father had been brought up in the depression and his family found it necessary to walk away from their 500 acre farm with literally the clothes on their backs. As a result, he learned that saving for a rainy day had much merit and was conservative in spending. Kate's mother, on the other hand, was part of a very wealthy family. She had been chauffeured all of her life until age 30 when Kate's mom learned she would now have to drive her own car. This upset her even to shedding tears. The different backgrounds in which her parents were raised actually gave Kate a healthy balance in regard to money. Both of her parents became good investors and taught Kate to do the same.

Kate's love for horses continued. She still had her pony in North Carolina and would see the pony during the summer when she visited her relatives. But now she had her horse as well. She walked to the stables every day to ride her horse. Her mom picked her up every evening and they'd stop by a fast food chain to pick up some dinner on the way home, then it was time for homework (Kate was a very good student). Her mother would drink and be lost in her own world, so there was always a level of pain from not having a parent who was really there. Kate also felt jealousy from her mom due to her relationship with her dad.

Kate spent as much time away from her house as was possible. Every day found her riding her horse and taking care of him. She practiced and trained and became an accomplished equestrian, winning many horse shows. Her parents supported her financially and attended her shows. It was during this time that some of the girls at the stables offered her a joint of marijuana to smoke. She refused at first but they kept after her, making fun of her for not being one of them. So she tried it. She noticed that a calmness came over her that she hadn't felt before, and the pain she felt from the lack of love in her life seemed to vanish, temporarily. Thus began a new path of self-destruction that would take Kate on a downward spiral for many years.

Smoking joints became Kate's way of life. It eased her pain and loneliness. By age ten she was hooked. Her grades fell and her priorities changed. No longer could she focus on academics as she had before. She was going to a private school where she could pick her classes, so she often simply skipped, and her grades continued to plummet. By now she was dropping acid as well.

Why did she resort to this lifestyle? She was so young. Kate said that she always had a deep-rooted anxiety in her stomach that would never go away. She didn't feel comfortable in her own skin. She always thought there was something wrong with her. Smoking a joint created a sort of euphoria, but more than that, it erased the anxiety and she would feel good in her skin. She would become more out-going and generally felt better. She could escape the pain and longing of what was lacking with her parents. And she was accepted by her peers.

Kate attended a party and smoked pot with the others present. Someone at the party told her aunt and uncle, and they drove all the way to Atlanta from South Carolina to inform her parents. Her parents were shaken and very upset.

She promised her parents she wouldn't do it again after seeing her dad cry, something she had not seen before. She stayed clean for three months.

One day at school, Kate saw a girl walking and noticed that every one of her fingernails were painted a different color. She thought that weird and decided she didn't like that girl. But somehow, a few days later, they ended up eating lunch together, and she and the girl, Jennifer, became great friends. In fact, they have remained friends to this day. They were thirteen at the time, and hung out together every day. However, when Jennifer was fifteen, her parents sent her to boarding school, which was hard on Kate. They visited each other from time to time, back and forth to their different schools, but it wasn't the same. However, their lives continued to weave in and out for many years until the day they found themselves nearby in the same city.

Kate didn't keep her promise to her parents. Three months after giving her word to never do drugs again, she went back into the drug scene. By twelve she had used LSD, MDA (speed hallucinogenic), and cocaine. Kate was kicked out of school. She found a job in a restaurant and had a boyfriend. She began hanging out with thirty-year-olds and somehow was slipped into bars with them. As a teenager, she remembers getting ready to walk out her door and her mom would say, "Where are you going?" She would reply "I'm going to get stoned" as she carried out a bag of pot. One time, her mom actually said, "Maybe I'll try one sometime." Nothing more was said so she simply walked out the door to her friends. This was in the 1970's, and there was a lot of media publicity stating that pot didn't lead to other drug usage. Because he had his own apartment, Kate stayed with her boyfriend most of the time so was rarely home.

One night, when Kate was going through the changes of puberty, she was getting ready to go out. Her mom suddenly asked Kate to hug her, mentioning how pretty she looked. This was very unusual and Kate refused. She asked again, but Kate still refused; something didn't feel right. Kate did not trust her mother. Her thoughts went back to the time when she was little and her mom had told her to come to the end of the dock to see a fish. Kate was afraid of the ocean then and wouldn't go see. Besides, the docks were far out so boats could tie down in deeper water. But she insisted, so Kate walked over to see the fish. Her mom reached out and pushed her into the water. Kate was petrified and cried as she swam all the way back to shore, all the while hearing her mother's laughter directed to her. Kate's thoughts returned to her mom's request again for a hug. Finally, Kate walked over to her, still wondering what was going on. Her mom grabbed Kate and began fondling her breasts. Kate was so angry and told her mom she was gross. Immediately she ran out the door and went out to find drugs.

At seventeen she got a job in a health store. She worked there for a while until it was turned into a bar. Now eighteen, she stayed on and worked at the bar. Consuming large amounts of drugs every day was Kate's way of life. In addition, she was selling drugs and making a great deal of money. Her dad was concerned but didn't pick up on the whole picture; he didn't realize she was doing so many drugs. Kate was living with a wealthy man who was much older than her; he was providing her with the drugs. She had been busted and stayed in jail overnight, and it was this man who bailed her out. One night he realized she was doing too much cocaine and told her to leave. She wanted to date others anyhow, so she took off. She was sexually active as it was a way for her to feel love, physically touched, and be nurtured.

Then Ted came along, a drug dealer. Kate was twenty and fell in love. She could talk to him in depth and they established a deep bond. Ted would travel to Bogata, and flight attendants on a well-known airline would smuggle the vast amount of drugs on the flights. There were kilos and kilos of cocaine on these flights. When Kate's parents were out of town, huge tractor-trailers would pull up to her house and drop off the bales of marijuana and kilos of cocaine. This was quickly bagged and sold and nothing was ever discovered by her parents.

Ted and Kate spent ten days in a hotel, and Kate consumed cocaine and alcohol non-stop with no food. Kate's parents were away, but she suddenly demanded that Ted take her home. She went inside of her home and laid down on her bed to sleep. But some time later she woke up outside in the front yard with Ted holding her; she had had a seizure. Paramedics came and took her to the hospital; she was having trouble breathing. It was then her dad realized the depth of her involvement with drugs, for before he had been in denial. Kate remembers thinking, "I just did too much." Kate overdosed again, and woke up in the hospital once more, this time with tubes sticking out of her. Nurses were assigned to her 24 hours; she almost didn't make it.

Once again, Kate thought, "I just did too much this time." There was no realization that she had a problem and needed help. Kate deeply loved Ted, and after yet another overdose, Ted told her she had to make a choice: Either him or the cocaine. This made Kate mad, so she went out with another guy, got stoned on drugs, and was sexually involved with him. When she came around to thinking more clearly, she became disgusted with herself, for she truly loved Ted. She had found a note on her car from Ted saying, "Where are you? I can't find you." Kate realized she was becoming like her mom, something she did not want to become. It wasn't alcohol that was her demon, but the drugs were just the same, for they took her out of reality into a world of illusion.

Later, after she arrived home, her dad knocked on her door, asking her to open the door so he could see if she was okay. She refused. So her dad went to her window outside and knocked on the window, saying, "Please just pull the drapes back so I can see that you are okay." Again she refused. No way was she going to let her dad see what she looked like at that moment because he'd know instantly she wasn't okay. After sleeping all day, she went out on her beautiful deck where a couple trees were actually growing through the deck in their natural state, and got down on her knees, and asked God to help her. Then she called her dad and Ted and asked for help.

The next day found Kate in a treatment center for drug addiction. She went to a Young Adult Treatment Unit and began a journey of healing. She was able to share her experience of sexual abuse from her mother and get honest about the feelings she experienced concerning that encounter. However, when she mentioned it to her mom, her mom's reply was "You're crazy. You made all this up. I'll disinherit you!" But Kate continued her work to heal.

A doctor on staff at the unit, Dr. Temples, was a wonderful person for Kate, and helped her tremendously. Kate worked hard, participating in single therapy as well as group therapy. During some of her therapy sessions, she experienced what many call an out-of-body experience. She felt as if she was suspended in space and pivoting within her body. She often had visions, feelings and messages from beings in the spirit world. Kate had great admiration and respect for Dr. Temples and how he worked with her. He commented that her mother was the one who needed to be in his therapy sessions, but since this was how it was and Kate sat in front of him, he would do all he could to protect and help her. She spent four months in this Young Adult Treatment Center. A vast amount of support and love flowed to Kate on her healing journey.

Kate knew a woman who was loud, obnoxious, an in-your-face kind of person, rather unkempt and not the cleanest person. Not long after leaving the Young Adult Center she ran into this woman. She could hardly believe what she saw. This woman glowed from within and looked absolutely beautiful. She had lost weight, cleaned herself up, and appeared the picture of great health. It was an amazing metamorphosis of this woman. They talked for a while, and this woman shared about a place of support that she attends. She took Kate to this place and it proved to be a wonderful life support in her life. Kate was on her way to a better life, a life without drugs.

Her boyfriend, Ted, had visited her often while she stayed in the Young Adult Treatment Center. Kate learned he had done a big drug deal and had the FBI looking for him, so they had to be careful seeing each other. Kate had her own apartment in Buckhead and was getting ready to go back to school and obtain her GED. One day, Ted called Kate and said he wanted to get clean, that he was going to turn himself in and change his life. She was overjoyed and excited. He even went so far as to suggest they get married and raise a family. It felt so good that Ted wanted to stop his life of self-destruction. Kate would think at times about the contradictory life she was living. "I'm clean," she thought, "living this really good life and getting myself back together, yet I'm with someone who still sells drugs." In 1987, Ted was murdered—two bullets in the head over a drug deal that went sour.

In the meantime, Kate had become quite psychic. Working with a woman named Joyce Rennolds, she studied various healing techniques such as Ro-hun therapy. She had a strong Kundalini experience as well, and continued to pursue the realm of spirit. But the death of her beloved Ted was a hard pill to swallow, and on top of that, due to Kate's past sexual activities, she was tested for HIV. She was so afraid of the possibility it would be positive that she actually thought she might consider killing herself if it was positive. She had a gun nearby just in case. But on this particular night, she went

And Now Kate's Story

into a telepathic state and talked to her dad, telling him how much she was hurting and that if her HIV test is positive she might kill herself.

The next day at noon, Kate's dad showed up at her apartment and asked her to lunch. They had a good time together and as they were about to part, her dad asked her for the guns. Wow! That meant her dad had received her message telepathically. Shortly after their meeting, she again told her dad telepathically that she wanted to drop out of college and attend a spiritual college. She mentioned her intense psychic experiences and didn't know how to work with them. Kate's dad drove to Atlanta without calling her, which confirmed Kate's telepathic abilities. Her dad told her she could go but she'd have to pay for this herself. Once again, she had been successful reaching her dad telepathically.

Kate registered for her new college, Delphi University, owned by Patricia Haynes. Kate loved this school and studied mediumship, Ro-hun, meditation, and special cultures. Her studies included travel to Brazil, Egypt, and Greece. This resonated with Kate in amazing ways.

During this time, Kate met a man—six foot three, brilliant, handsome, a black belt—and fell madly in love. They lived together a year before getting married. It was every girl's dream wedding, huge and plush, with 500 people attending. Yet the night before the wedding, her husband-to-be hit her. A big red flag waved in front of Kate but she overlooked it, thinking it might just be the pre-wedding stress. There were other occurrences, and the couple began counseling. However, when the abuse continued, Kate chose not to live this way and divorced her husband. After the divorce, she learned that domestic violence is often demonstrated by people who appear as the nicest people on the outside. That makes it hard for others to believe they are violent, so it makes the accuser appear to be a liar.

On the rebound, Kate rekindled a relationship with Bruce, someone she had known since she was a teenager. She asked about his whereabouts. Tracking down his dad, Kate discovered Bruce was in jail. She began writing to him in jail, and when he was released she married him. Bruce had been incarcerated for drug trafficking.

Kate and Bruce had been involved on and off for many years. Kate thought back to a time when Bruce had helped her when she needed some loving attention. She had been clean for about three months, when she was 25 years old, and as she was getting into her car a black guy jumped in wanting money. He attempted to rape her, and then attempted to strangle her, but Kate screamed at the top of her lungs. The disturbance gave her a moment to try to escape. But he grabbed her long hair and pulled her back, dragging her across the street, almost running over her with her car. She was so terrified she wet her pants. She made a run for it and was able to finally escape. The guy took off in her car and she sought help. The police were called. The mark on her neck verified she was almost strangled. She called Ted but he was on the run so was not available for her.

Somehow, Bruce found out about what happened and contacted Kate, wanting to help her. He took her to his parent's home where she was nurtured and pampered. Kate was afraid to be alone so this was just what she needed. Their kindness and love was accepted and appreciated.

Kate went to court and learned the guy who attempted to rape her had tried the same thing with two other girls. This was 1985, and in the judicial system there was a struggle for balance between the white and black races. Jurors said that white girls and white detectives were framing the black guy. Kate's past was revealed which made her look like trash. The entire experience felt ugly. In fact, Kate felt more raped by the court experience than the guy's actual attempt. They let him go and dismissed the charges from Kate and another girl, but he was made accountable for the charges of one girl with whom he did complete the rape.

Shortly after this event, Kate began working in a spiritual center. She loved working there and was doing readings for people. She had been away from drugs for seven years, was married to Bruce and now pregnant, and living a life she'd always dreamed of. Life seemed good. Bruce had been a drug dealer in the past but had stopped dealing. But suddenly Bruce began buying things for Kate, anything she touched, no matter the cost, he would buy for her. Red flags were waving all over the place and Kate suspected he'd gone back to dealing drugs. Kate said to God, "I think something is going on. Please show me the truth." One day, Kate walked outside just as Bruce opened the trunk and she saw the trunk full of Tai-sticks. This is marijuana wrapped around a stick, and looks like something was sprayed on the stick. It is very potent and creates strong hallucinations. Every time Kate asked God to show her the truth, she would find the drugs. Kate was scared, so she separated from Bruce.

Bruce promised he'd quit dealing and pull his life together. Kate so wanted to believe him but she had her doubts. She sought the advice of her attorney who told her she could not stay with Bruce. The attorney reminded her of her arrests and said if anything happened and she was implicated, she could lose her house and even her child. The divorce was heartbreaking because she really loved Bruce, but she knew she had to protect herself and her baby. Besides, she was working at a treatment center with adolescents who were healing from drug use, so how could she stay with someone who was dealing drugs. It just couldn't work.

Kate worked at the treatment center until just before her baby was born. Bruce remained in her and their daughter, Nicole's, life. Bruce kept her yard maintained beautifully, gave her plenty of child support money, and they stayed together on weekends so they could enjoy their daughter together. It was a beautiful time and they shared many enjoyable memories. However, Kate's immune system was not functioning as it should. She began having debilitating migraines and multiple sinus infections. Seeking medical help, it was suggested she be tested for allergies, which she did. Allergy shots began but they didn't offer her any relief. She was living on antibiotics and steroids, and ended up using these for years. She reached a point in which she was so sick she couldn't take care of her daughter, and at one point ended up in the hospital, but fortunately she had employed a nanny who took good care of Nicole. Kate had trouble even standing or walking and was pathetically thin. Bouts of excruciating pain, bladder problems and infections, and multiple excursions to the hospital continued for months. One doctor suggested endoscopic sinus surgery. She had the surgery, but the pain and infections continued. Finally, the doctors told her they couldn't help her. What was she to do?

The migraines continued along with lots of meds to help control the pain, often requiring a trip to the hospital for more meds. Sometimes she had to wait for hours to be seen. She was sick of all this and didn't have any idea where to turn for help. One time, however, Bruce was with her and had some heroin. He told her to try it and see if it helped. It did, and shortly the pain was gone. No more trips to the hospital and waiting for hours in so much pain. So she kept some heroin around for times when a migraine hit.

For six months she only used the heroin when a migraine came on. Then she crossed the line, and in 1996, began using heroin all the time. This continued for two years, but because it is so costly, she used needles. By using needles you could use a smaller amount yet get really high. She had reached a point where she couldn't function without her fix. Kate made a lot of money in the stock market, but she went through $50,000.00 very quickly paying for the heroin.

This went on for two years, then it was off to another treatment facility. This was a horrible experience for Kate. Withdrawal from heroin causes excruciating pain. She likened the pain to being in labor for two weeks straight, due to the intense abdominal pain. It takes two weeks to detoxify your body from the heroin. Kate struggled for five years to remain clean. She found another support group which helped her tremendously. She had had eleven years clean, then went back out again. It was a continuous battle that took her in and out of drug use.

Working with the support group gave her an added benefit. She met a man who was also recovering from drug addiction. They dated, fell in love, and were married. Since Bruce, Nicole's father, was strung out on drugs, Kate's third husband thought it would be good for him to adopt Nicole. Amazingly, Bruce agreed to this. But Kate's heart sank when not long after their wedding, her husband relapsed and she realized she had allowed a man to adopt her daughter who went back out on drugs. She was pregnant again, yet her heart was breaking. She saw the similarity to her previous pregnancy and the subsequent disappointment when she discovered her husband had relapsed back into drugs.

Her husband was being dishonest and wasn't there for her, and he actually began seeing an old girlfriend. Kate was six months pregnant and in a great deal of emotional pain with all that was going on in her life. When she found drugs in his car, she would flush them down the toilet. This happened repeatedly and it made her feel angry and hurt. In her pain, Kate decided to take just a little bit of heroin. It helped, for a moment. Then Kate realized she was mirroring her mom. She also realized that none of the guys she had picked were there for her, just like her mom hadn't been. She thought about these people who on some level were really great individuals, but just couldn't get it together. This realization was very disheartening to Kate.

And Now Kate's Story

Kate thought back to a time when she was in a session with her therapist. The therapist asked, "Why do you think your mom is as she is?" At that moment, Kate had an awareness that her mom had been molested by at least one parent. Tears began streaming down Kate's face as she thought of this beautiful, angelic child, growing up in a wealthy, affluent environment, and being severely abused. Kate remembered her grandmother being mean and demeaning to all of them as she had probably been to her mom, and remembered that her grandmother had tried to lift her shirt and look at her breasts once. Kate felt love and compassion for her mom which she had never felt before. How could she hate someone who had endured something like that? It gave Kate a new understanding of her mom and her mom's behavior.

Kate remembered one time at the Young Adult Treatment Center, how she received this thought about her mom. She actually wished she could swallow a grenade and stand next to her mom, allowing the grenade to explode and splat all over her mom – she hated her that much at that time. Kate said it wasn't the inappropriate sexual behavior that hurt so much even though she thought it gross, but it was the fact that her own mother would scapegoat her and not tell the truth. That infuriated Kate. Her mom always would say, "You're a crazy drug addict. You have a vivid imagination." This is what hurt so much.

Kate used heroin only once during her last trimester; she stayed clean for the sake of her baby. Kate began having strange cramps that were not like the typical labor pains. She went to the emergency room and the doctor said some-

{ 253 }

thing was wrong, that the baby's heart rate was very low. She was prepped for an emergency C-section and an epidural was injected. But it didn't take. Kate could feel everything, yet there was no time to wait. Kate screamed with the pain as the doctors had to proceed cutting her without anything for her pain. She said it felt as if someone was inside her and squeezing and twisting her intestines, and it burned. She had never felt any pain like this before. It was indescribable. Once her son, Gage, was out they gave her medication and the pain subsided. But her son wasn't breathing well and they discovered he had meconium aspirations (waste matter in his lungs). He was put on machines that did everything for him until the waste matter could be released from his body. He remained in ICU for two months.

Kate came home to a house aflutter with drugs. Her husband was using again and it was hard for Kate to resist. The day she came home from the treatment center for the second time, he said he had something called ecstasy. He told her he had saved it until she got home because it was very sexual and he wanted to do it with her. She refused, thinking how desperately she was trying to get clean and stay clean. But he kept insisting she try it with him. Since she was having some withdraw, she tried it. Later she tried cactus and mushrooms as well. When Gage was one year old, she placed herself into a treatment center called a halfway house. She didn't want to come home because she knew drugs would be there. She also knew that being around them was not good for her; it was too much of a temptation. The nanny she had hired took care of her two children. Now, she was again clean.

And Now Kate's Story

She had been clean again for three months when her parents took Kate and her husband to Jamaica to celebrate her mother's eightieth birthday. While there, she relapsed on cocaine with her husband. She was angry at herself for doing this again, and when he kept using she gathered all the drugs and drug paraphernalia and put them into a dirty diaper so he couldn't use it. She told her dad that she couldn't stay married to her husband if she wanted to stay clean. They hated the thought of her getting another divorce, but she decided it was necessary so she could stay clean.

While in Jamaica she was bitten by a spider and upon returning home was put in the hospital for two weeks. During her stay her husband called to tell her that Bruce, her second husband and Nicole's real dad, had overdosed and died. This was hard for Kate to handle. Bruce was a great friend and now he was gone. On top of that she was dealing with her own low self-worth issues and trying to save her marriage. She took some drugs, but shortly after doing that, she decided she wanted to get clean and stay clean. When she returned home after her final stint in a treatment center, she discovered that the $200,000.00 dollars she had in her account had been liquidated and was gone, and that none of her bills had been paid.

Kate taught school for a while but soon realized this wasn't for her. Ever since she was a child, she had collected rocks and stones. She was drawn to antique coral and bought some of it from time to time. She decided to apply for a job as a jewelry show host, but she didn't get the job. She wanted to move so put her house on the market and had received a contract, but suddenly the hurricane Katrina hit, and a large tree fell on the house, causing a great deal of damage. The contract fell through, and since her insurance company paid her well, she decided it was a sign to remain where she was. The house was remodeled, and she still lives there today.

Friends told her she should work with jewelry since she loves it so much. She bought a small case, filled it with jewelry, and proceeded to a place called Lakewood where she sold her jewelry. She did well there and found some dear friends who were very supportive. One couple, who has millions and millions of dollars worth of jewelry, have guns to protect themselves as they are placing their jewelry in a safe after a show. They escort Kate when she places her jewelry into the safe as well, protecting her. They often all eat together and enjoy fun times. Kate feels very blessed and protected. It's a company with which she loves to work. She has studied gemology through reading many books and then simply became involved with the hands-on approach of learning.

The pattern of abuse and addiction that Kate experienced as a child and continued into her adult life, is a pattern she has now broken. She continued that same pattern of abuse and addiction with the three marriages she had, but now she sees this pattern and has torn it up and tossed it out. No more abuse. No more addiction. She simply made the choice to get help and be free from the bonds of addiction. And her life has made a tremendous metamorphosis as she has become the beautiful butterfly, flying free. She loves how Spirit guides her on her daily path.

Kate's desire is that you take these thoughts from her story: "Know that no matter what you've gone through, your life can change into what you really desire. I doubt anyone says 'I want to be a drug addict when I grow up,' or 'When I grow up I want to totally screw up my life.' So, know that no matter what you've endured as a child, you can grow up to be a radiant, healthy, happy, abundant person having a great life."

IN KATE'S WORDS

I LOOK AT MY BEAUTIFUL CHILDREN, Gage and Nicole, and I feel so blessed to be their mother. They are cute, healthy, happy, bright and very spiritual. In fact, both are gifted healers. I thank God every day for the gift of these children. Our home is filled with love, support, and lots of laughter.

My business is Ubiquity. I absolutely love this business as I am able to buy and sell both antique and estate jewelry. I have collected gem stones and jewelry since I was a child and am passionate about it. Through my business contacts I have been blessed to meet wonderful people who are also in the jewelry business; they have enhanced my life greatly. In addition, I feel passionate about helping people heal their lives and fulfill their dreams. As I have been on my own healing journey, many extraordinary people have crossed my path and blessed my life.

My family and friends are the best in the entire universe. We've had problems, but there was always a solution. Having such a big problem with addiction, I learned along my

{ 257 }

journey that there is a vast wealth of support available in the community, and it was those wonderful, supportive people that actually saved my life. To them I am most grateful.

I now live my life to the best of my ability by spiritual laws and principles. I believe this is the key to living a life that is filled with love and abundance. Every day is a grand adventure and the same can be true for you. I send my love to you with a wish that you too can find all that is for your highest and greatest good.

I wish to express gratitude to Joyce Rennolds, Jennifer Wadsworth, Cyla Nelson, and Eric Jennings because they have taught me to live by spiritual laws and principles rather than the earthly laws that ruled my life before. I live in the midst of abundance, love and beauty every day of my life now. Without a doubt, I am living my bliss and have the life I've always desired, and it just keeps getting better and better!

Epilogue

Kate lives with her children and has a beautiful life now. She's been clean for five years and has chosen to remain completely clean. She feels her children deserve to be loved and cared for by her and she is committed to that.

One of her most favorite times is when an individual comes to her with pain and hurt in their eyes, but after working with her they understand things differently, and their eyes glow and sparkle because she could help them. She says it is such a wonderful feeling, true ecstasy.

Kate and her mom have established a wonderful relationship. Her mom has come a long way over the years. Without a doubt, Kate's parents have been there for her through everything in the best way they could. For their support during her trying times, she is grateful.

You can contact Kate at gagek@bellsouth.net or call her at (404) 556-7490.

Afterword

As you reflect back on these stories, the challenges, the efforts to overcome, the fortitude that prevailed, and the triumph over seeming insurmountable odds, realize these ordinary people are no different from you. Whatever challenge you might be facing, you can create a new story and step out of your old story of pain, suffering, heartache, struggle and apparent tragedy. How do you do this? After all, your life story is unique and has different challenges.

Throughout all of these stories there are some common denominators for how these individuals conquered what life dealt them. As I define them for you, understand that these same strengths are within you, enabling you to accomplish a victory. The most powerful common denominator between each individual is that they left their old story behind. It is the power of choice!

The first quality that is vital to overcome anything is this: *Never give up!* No matter what appears in your life, it is there for a reason, and you have both the strength and ability to step over it and become a better and stronger person for experiencing it. Another thought is that you must have *perseverance.*

Secondly, each person knew deep within *that they could make it* through their challenge. Perhaps it was their faith in God that allowed this strength. Defeat wasn't an option, even if it took them some time to see that. Their determination was strong. It was simply time to regroup, restructure, rebuild, and renew their life. In other words, they would eventually make lemonade out of the sour lemons they received because inside they knew there was a way.

Even if it was not evident in the beginning, the third concept each of these people eventually understood is that there was *a bigger picture* to their challenge. When an individual experiences a shock or challenge, they are in the middle of a problematic situation and it is often hard to understand there is a greater picture. But there always is, and as time goes by each person will appreciate more fully the reason for this challenge. As often happens, the difficulty was necessary so the individual could make a shift into a new level of awareness that wasn't evident before. And the bigger picture always includes a way to give back to the world in some way, perhaps to help others as they face their challenge and need support from you and people like you so they can make it through. *The key to moving through the challenge with ease is to simply flow with the current instead of fighting it.*

Where are you in your life right now? Are you experiencing a heavy burden that keeps you stumbling and sometimes falling to the ground? Get up! You can do it! You have the strength within you and the power to overcome anything—yes, anything! So how do you do this? How do you fight the defeat, doubt, lack, hurt, pain, depression, anger and resentment you feel inside? Let me share some steps with you to help guide you on your path to *becoming the victor.*

Your first step is the hardest: *Decide you want something better in your life.* You might be saying "Of course I want something better." But do you really? Are you simply saying the words but do not believe it in your heart? This is the decision-making point for most individuals. They know the right words, can recite them easily whenever necessary, and may even tell themselves they believe them, but if their heart doesn't know it as a truth they are sabotaging their own forward movement. People are so good at self-sabotage because their thought usually sounds good and is justified according to their perception. It might go like this. You've been guided to step away from your present relationship because it isn't raising you into a higher plane, but you are afraid you might be alone or that you won't have financial security, so you remain in misery. You've been nudged to write a book but doubt you can find the time or resources to do it, so ignore the idea. You feel led to open a new business but friends and family are discouraging you because it takes hard work, money, and much planning, and they see your life as okay as it is. Perhaps you've heard that inner voice ask you to begin a new vocation, one that frightens you and you don't feel you can do, so you push it into the background, hoping it will go away. It's often hard to make the decision to let go of the things presently in front of you and move into new territory. This is why the hardest step is always the first, and relinquishing your safe position on top of the fence may be your hardest decision. You must make a choice.

Step two: *Define what you want.* You made a choice for something better. What exactly do you want? Most people spend their time focusing on what they don't want, what they don't like, what isn't working. Instead, focus on what you want so it can show up in your life. *Your thoughts create your life experiences—always remember this truth!*

Society is constantly focusing on the negative—the "bad" things that happen. All you have to do is watch the first few minutes of the news and you'll understand the mode of fear. When a challenge enters your life, what do you focus on? Perhaps your desire is to own your own home but your finances are not in a place that are allowing that to happen. Maybe you've been struggling financially all your life up to this point. Instead of focusing on the money you don't have or the fact that you have to live where you are, begin seeing the house you want. Imagine what it would feel like to live in it, and do some positive things with the money you presently have: pay off bills, curb your spending, save some dollars every week towards the house, and by all means change your thoughts into knowing a house IS obtainable. Also, be grateful for all you presently have and even for the challenge you are experiencing for you are blessed already if you just see it. Defining what you want is simply placing an intention (thought) out to God and the universe and believing it will come to you.

Step three: *Surrender and get out of the way!* This is so difficult for most people to do since our human nature is to grab the controls and run the show. But once you've placed an intention or thought of what you want to the universe, the best and easiest way for it to reach you is by getting out of the way and not working out any details. Sliding into the passenger's seat requires letting go (surrender) of the steering wheel—not something easily done by the control freaks of this world. What I learned along my journey is that anything that is in alignment with our spirit is an effortless undertaking. It doesn't mean we don't have to work at it. It simply means we don't have to manipulate or force it to occur in any way; we simply allow it to flow to us. As you patiently wait for the unfolding of your desire, keep your vision alive by focusing on it and not the external circumstances around you that may not give any evidence it is in the process of appearing.

Step four: *Be willing to move forward through the doors that open.* Many times individuals say they want to find new direction and are looking for something better, but when the doors open are afraid and hold back, not willing to take that step into the unknown. This might look like remaining in a going nowhere job because it pays the bills and you are afraid a new job might not provide sufficient income. Or you tell yourself the relationship you're in is okay, better than others you know, even though it is totally non-nurturing, stale, and wilting.

So when a new door opens that is unfamiliar and frightening, remember that you will only be given doors to walk through in which you have the ability to succeed. More than likely, the doors that open are the direct response to your thoughts, with or without your conscious knowledge. Somewhere, at some time, you had a thought that brought to you your present opportunity. Perhaps you entertained the thought of a new career in a particular area but never pursued it. However, the universe heard that desire and began ushering in the steps that led your company to downsize, leaving you without a job. With no job, you are wide open to begin that other career you thought about months earlier. Step four is simply being willing to accept the opportunity and run with it.

Step five: *Be grateful for the fulfillment of your desire before it shows up!* This is a very important aspect of receiving the desires of your heart. It shows you believe in your own power of aligning with the universal energy that creates your life experiences as you desire them to be. Living in the state of thankfulness allows you to be constantly happy no matter what is going on in your external life. This state allows you to see the good, to feel and see your present abundance, and know that as you focus on the good, more will continue to show up.

What I learned along my journey has completely transformed my life in every aspect of it. Learning that I was born worthy of all good and didn't have to do anything to earn it was a life-changing realization. Once I understood my birthright I could understand the value of every person on this planet. As I understood the power of my heritage and that I had no limits except in my own mind, I could grasp more easily the magnitude of my own power when connected to God my Source. The incredible part of these realizations is that this is true for everyone. Each one of you reading this book has the same power to create what you want in your life. In addition, you have the power to do what you think is impossible: you can change the world!

Each person who shared their story has learned many things along their journey. One thing they learned is the power of forgiveness. Forgiveness is an expression of love and only love can heal. Situations, people, and pain that showed up in each person's life required forgiveness, not just for others, but for themselves. When there is no forgiveness, there is blame, anger, frustration, resentment, bitterness, rejection, abandonment, and self incrimination. These negative emotions are all based in fear and create unfavorable results in your life. Forgiveness is an expression of God. God expresses as love. Remember this: *only love heals.* In every story you can see the emergence of love so a victory could occur.

As you reflect on the stories shared in this book, notice how these individuals forged ahead in spite of their difficulties. Each story reflects a realization of something bigger, something more grandiose than their own problems, and it involves a knowing that what they learned along their journey is to be shared with the world. Each of us can make a difference in this wonderful world of ours and it is actually our responsibility to step up to the plate and do it.

So, at this very moment, I ask you to stop and think about your life. Where are you going? Are you moving at all or are you stuck in the spot where you are right now? Do you have aspirations that you've discarded and hidden perhaps even from yourself? Are you still playing the victim role and feeling your life a total drag?

Emmet Fox made this statement that completes my thoughts for the purpose of this book and our life experiences: "It is the Law that any difficulties that can come to you at any time, no matter what they are, must be exactly what you need most at the moment, to enable you to take the next step forward by overcoming them. The only real misfortune, the only true tragedy, comes when we suffer without learning the lesson."

You have a phenomenal power of choice. In fact, it is up to you to create your tomorrow right now. Don't continue on the roller coaster ride you've been riding. *Only you can change it.* Anything you want is right before you; you simply must believe in it and allow it in. Henry Ford believed it. Christopher Columbus believed it. Mother Theresa believed it. All of the people in these stories used their power of choice, some sooner than others. Their choice was to rise above the challenge and become greater, rather than remaining in a place of smallness. In the process of emerging into a higher realm, they created amazing things in their life. Was it because they had all the breaks given to them? No, not at all. Instead they learned to persevere no matter what because they knew they could. They accepted and overcame their obstacle because they decided to do so. Then, in total humility, they knew their purpose on earth involved making a difference in our world.

Now you have a choice—to either remain where you are or rise above any challenge and see it as a great gift in your life. Don't get discouraged no matter how long it takes to move through it because you can do it if you believe you can. If you believe you can, or if you believe you can't, you are right! It's all up to you. You too have the power and capability to create your own Road to Glory!

About the Author

Carolyn Porter, D. Div., an internationally recognized Author, Spiritual Wholeness Coach, Speaker, Trainer, and owner of Where Miracles Happen healing center, has dedicated her life to helping others understand their inborn power and magnificence to create the life they truly want to live. Divinely guided, she put together this book so that individuals can move beyond their struggles and fears to create what they can dream is possible.

Although receiving a Bachelor of Science in Music Education was a first step in her life's work, Carolyn was later guided to obtain a Masters and Doctorate of Divinity. She is the owner of Empower Productions, Inc. and is also co-founder and co-owner of the All About Health store. Recently, she opened her own healing center in Woodstock, Georgia—Where Miracles Happen.

Carolyn's books and insights have been shared on radio, TV and print media throughout the United States as well as internationally. She continues to offer hope to those who seek a better life through the spiritual principles she teaches. Carolyn offers workshops, trainings, private sessions, wholeness coaching for health, life direction, spiritual empowerment, and self-publishing a book. To sign up for Carolyn's free enewsletter, receive her free ebook, contact her for a personal session, or learn more about her work, visit www.drcarolynporter.com.

A mother of five—two sons and three daughters—Carolyn resides in Woodstock, Georgia.